A V A N T

G A R D E

PHOTOGRAPHY

IN GERMANY

1919·1939

AVANT GARDE PHOTOGRAPHY IN GERMANY 1919·1939

VAN DEREN COKE

PANTHEON BOOKS
NEW YORK

Library of Congress Cataloging in Publication Data

Coke, Van Deren, 1921–
   Avant-garde photography in Germany, 1919–1939.
    1. Photography— Germany— History.   2. Photography
— Germany— History— Exhibitions.   I. Title.
TR73.C64   779'.0943'074   81-22300
ISBN 0-394-52522-1   AACR2
ISBN 0-394-71052-5 (pbk.)

Designed by Naomi Osnos
Manufactured in West Germany
First American Edition

CONTENTS

P R E F A C E

This book is intended to serve as an introduction to the work of the photographers who contributed so much to the development of a new vision in Germany in the 1920s. The text is an expansion of the introduction to a catalog of the same title published by the San Francisco Museum of Modern Art (Henry Hopkins, director). For his encouragement I want to express deep appreciation. Many other individuals and institutions helped to make this book possible. Especially helpful in Germany were Ute Eskildsen, Essen; Bernd Lohse, Leverkusen; Rudolf Kicken, Cologne; and Hans Georg Puttnies, Frankfurt. In the United States, Dorothy Martinson, San Francisco; Robert Shapazian, Fresno; Eugene Prakapas, New York City; Steven White, Los Angeles; and Gerd Sander, Washington, D.C., have all been very helpful, and I am most appreciative.

Further, I wish to express my appreciation to the photographers, museums, collectors, and dealers who permitted me to reproduce photographs from their collections.

Van Deren Coke
January 1982

AVANT-GARDE PHOTOGRAPHY IN GERMANY, 1919 – 1939

In the 1920s a new breed of photographers in tune with the very successful world of German technology and Germany's turbulent political situation overturned many of the major traditions of their medium. Photography, as an artistic medium and respected profession serving commerce and the need for reportage and portraiture, took on new meaning. A sense of confidence replaced Germany's old, incapacitating inferiority complex. Avant-garde photographers in such major centers as Berlin, Munich, and Cologne explored the use of daring new ways to register on film the great changes taking place in the world. New uses were found for the camera's ability to record with exactitude the products of industry that were in need of introduction to the public. Photographers used their skills to foster new attitudes toward such diverse things as cool, modern architecture and the influence of Freud and the world of dreams. A feeling of experimental freedom prevailed in Germany and opened for the first time new ways for photographers to explore their emotions and everything they saw going on around them.

The first question one might ask is why new ideas came from Germany at the end of World War I when Germany had been defeated in a devastating war that caused great suffering and severe political disruptions. Why not from France and England, the victorious countries in 1918? One of the reasons was that the French and English felt that their vaunted heritages had played a major role in bringing about victory, and with complacency they relied to a large degree on the inspiration of the past in dealing with the new world that developed after the war. For Germans the past had lost its attraction. To understand this we must go back to the turn of the century, when Germany was fast becoming a major political power as well as an industrial nation of first rank. It must be recalled that Germany developed from a group of independent states into a unified nation only after 1870. At this time German nationalism began to stir due to the success of the army at Sedan, where the French were defeated in the Franco-Prussian War and Napoleon III was captured on the field of battle. By the time World War I began in August 1914, Germany had consolidated her position as a major manufacturing nation and world power with a very modern army and navy. When hostilities began, the country's efficient factories were converted to produce all kinds of war goods. Great strides were made in steel and chemical production–both keys to success in war–and it appeared to her people that Germany's army would again be victorious. Defeat came instead, in November 1918.

In 1919 the Germans began to see themselves as righteous victims of a system they had believed in but that had failed them. It was generally felt that the war had been forced on them, and defeat had been caused by political leaders who were overly sure of themselves due to the success of the post-Franco-Prussian War period as well as other victories in the past. The sudden defeat in 1918 was very painful to accept. The disillusionment, along with the knowledge of the very high indemnities imposed by the Allies in the Treaty of Versailles, caused a downtrodden feeling among the German people. After a disastrous period of runaway inflation and severe political tensions, however, the Weimar Republic established a state of relative stability with money supplied by American and British banks. A brighter outlook began to prevail. The German people did not romanticize their hard lot or slump into passivity but faced up to their situation and looked to the future for release from the bondage brought about by defeat. The past had not served them well as a guide, so the present and immediate future were looked to for ideas that would again give them material comforts and bring emancipation from the yoke of the victors. That which was new or had a veneer of newness became, for psychological reasons, very much in vogue in Germany, whereas in France and England almost the opposite was true.

Out of the first »machine« war came the realization in Germany that the technology that produced bombers and tanks could be used to manufacture goods for a new society. Machines were redesigned to create simple but elegant kitchenware, light fixtures, and means of transportation. The emphasis placed on industrial architecture was clearly revealed in the nature of structural engineering, and there grew an interest on the part of artists and designers in the precision of cogs, pipes, the planes of ribbed aluminum, and the textures of other industrial materials.

Germany's modernist movement in photography, or »new vision« as it was often called, grew out of a heightened awareness of the aesthetic possibilities of geometric forms–either those related to the machine or to architecture.

This new kind of photography began to make its appearance in Germany, while most photographers in France and England continued to work very much as they had before World War I. As early as 1922 the medium began to function in Germany in a variety of areas such as advertising, marketing, and the popular press–areas inherently attuned to the expanded manufacturing and distribution systems that evolved. Photography in advertising was a new concept, as was photojournalism, which in contrast to simple newspaper photography only rarely conveyed the photographer's own responses to his or her subjects. The fast pace of modern life in Berlin, Munich, and Cologne fostered new approaches to photography as a language. Young adventuresome photographers tried new ideas in design and tested the relationship between type and photographs. They also developed new ways to make use of the amazing new cameras and fast film that were being introduced in the 1920s in Germany. Achievements in technology became the subject for a new breed of industrial photographers who made pictures for catalogs and posters. The photojournalist competed for space in popular periodicals with their interpretations of the complex and contradictory forces at work. They evoked both the dynamism of machines and people's faith in them and the fruitful future they seemed to symbolize. The new vision that was born in photography was successfully applied to portraiture as well as advertising and journalism. If we study the pictures created by this new vision by dozens of free-spirited photographers, we can construct a mental image, a kind of montage, of German life and thought in the 1920s. The hypnotic forces at work in this exciting period become apparent when one takes time to delve beneath the surface of these deft and precise pictures.

As is always the case with dramatic social movements, leaders emerge, and soon enough their followers then take over. In some cases these followers add to the new vision they themselves had only a minor role in creating.

The flag bearers in the campaign to establish the acceptance of the new vision in photography were László Moholy-Nagy and Albert Renger-Patzsch. They arrived on the scene early, had firm ideas about photography, and stated their views forcefully in print. Equally important was Dr. Erich Salomon, who originated a new kind of communication with the marvelous little Ermanox camera. Salomon's pictures were widely published, and they greatly influenced the development of what was to become photojournalism. It was Moholy, however, who most influenced photography as a creative means of expression.

Hungarian born, LASZLO MOHOLY-NAGY was wounded during World War I and turned to art while convalescing. After the war he was in touch with the dadaists and constructivists–first in Vienna and then in Berlin–from whom he adopted many of the ideas he eventually used in his work.

Moholy, although always a painter and designer, became the key figure in photography in Germany in the 1920s. As is well known, his work with the camera absorbed only a small portion of his energy. He also made daring light sculptures and films, was a graphic and stage designer, and became an inspiring teacher and writer. His photography, however, was probably the most original aspect of his life's work. In photography he saw ways to expand the range of visual language to respond to the times and to new ideas about light, space, and psychology. He seems to have understood intuitively that the medium could invest ordinary subject matter with new emotional and even metaphysical content consistent with concepts being formulated in other media. He felt that people had to abandon the accepted limits of photography and regard the camera and film as flexible means of using light to make images. The images he himself created, and those that continue to show his influence, assert–sometimes in a quiet fashion and other times in a dramatic one–the new experiences of moving by fast train or automobile and the perspective of looking down from an airplane, as well as the changes brought about by the new and widespread use of artificial illumination. These changes created in the 1920s a distinctly different environment, which in turn altered people's psychological relationships with their surroundings. Such changes, and the unsettled nature of society in Germany in the 1920s, produced emotional effects that had not yet appeared in photographs. Moholy's photographic imagery dealt subtly with the anxieties that grew out of the larger sense of apprehension experi-

enced in Germany in the exhilarating but threatening 1920s.

Moholy took the radical view that photography was the quintessential modern medium with which to deal with the psychological effects of the new environment and the new sense of space and time. Through his writings and the exhibition of his photography and photograms (cameraless imagery on photosensitive paper), he conferred on the medium of photography a legitimacy that had been denied earlier. The significance of his attitude and the range and innovativeness of his photography cannot be overestimated when we view the respected position attained by German photography in the 1920s and 1930s. His refreshing and all-embracing view of the medium's possibilities for artistic expression came out of the Bauhaus, which issued books reproducing his work.

Students at the Bauhaus and at other innovative design schools in Germany adapted the new photography to their experiments in graphic design, photojournalism, and advertising illustrations. The extensive exposure of Moholy's ideas in print and in exhibitions in Germany near the end of the 1920s and in other countries in the 1930s was of great importance to the international development of the new vision.

Simply stated, Moholy saw more than other people did and brought previously unperceived insights to the psychological effects of the photographic image. He saw the camera and photosensitive paper as means of expressing to the general public, in totally new ways, his response to his time.

The ideas introduced in the 1920s in Germany, which were a considerable departure from tradition, included shooting straight up or down and creating photograms. In addition, there were stop-action pictures made with small cameras, negative prints made to alter reality, extreme close-up portraits made to convey dramatic and psychological effects, and very sharp details of plants, animals, and minerals. Pictures were also being made by intentionally tilting the plane of the back of the camera, creating diagonal forms. Most of these new forms of photography were explored by Moholy. He understood that the camera narrows vision and can be used to deform shapes so that we see familiar things in a fresh and stimulating way.

On many levels Moholy was one of those rare people who sensed the new phenomena of the 1920s and chose the camera and photosensitive materials to deal with them. Especially important was his frequent use of strong diagonals. Because we are bilaterally symmetrical, we tend to reject diagonals, endeavoring to make forms parallel with the edges of pictures. A feeling of tension occurs when we encounter pictures that have strong diagonal elements. The anxiety created by this formal, visual device reflected what many people felt subliminally in Germany during this period of rapid change. That viewers could identify with the subjects in Moholy's photography made it easier for them to embrace and emotionally respond to the energies and anxieties beneath the surface of his nominal subjects. They could translate the language of photography into personal experience–something that many people found difficult to do when confronted by works done in other media focusing on the same phenomena. A grasp of the various ways Moholy's ideas were spread is important to a better understanding of his key role. One of the avenues of exposure to the new vision was large exhibitions where equipment and photographs were shown to the public. The history of these exhibitions must be outlined in some detail to give a clear picture of the very real importance of Germany's photography exhibitions and expositions and the acceptance of the innovations created by Moholy and the other new-vision photographers. There were many more large-scale photography exhibitions held in Germany in the period 1920-1933 than in any other country. The first one after World War I took place in Stuttgart.[1] »Deutsche Photographische Ausstellung« (German Photography Exhibition) was largely a trade fair. In conjunction with it,

however, an exhibition of pictorial photographs was shown in a local art museum. Since the turn of the century, the amateur pictorialist had dominated the medium. In 1925 the »Kino- und Photoausstellung« (Film and Photography Exhibition) opened in Berlin. The »Kipho« was divided into various areas, including a section organized by Erich Stenger on the historical development of film and photography.

The following year, 1926, the »Deutsche Photographische Ausstellung« opened in Frankfurt. Interest in this exhibition was stirred by a design competition for a poster announcing it. The magazine Das Atelier des Photographen (The Photographic Studio) published the poster designs of August Sander, Hugo Erfurth, Franz Grainer, and Franz Fiedler, among others. The majority of the designs submitted were traditionally pictorial in concept. One by Hugo Erfurth and W. Petzold, however, was very nearly abstract, and Franz Fiedler's positive/negative design also incorporated new concepts. In addition to film and photography works, examples of reprotechnology, amateur photography, scientific photography, and the work of professional photographers were included in this exhibition. The feature of the exhibition was the work of the Kleeblatt (Cloverleaf) group from Austria, which included Heinrich Kühn, Hans Watzek, and Hugo Henneberg. As an indication that the new-vision photographers had yet to receive recognition for their innovations, it should be noted that Moholy's work was included in the exhibition's »amateur« section. He took advantage of the opportunity afforded by the exhibition to comment on photography used for objective representation: »The emphasis is on presenting photographic elements. Controlling these elements can lead to a synthetic photographic achievement. These elements are, essentially, the possibility of creating unadulterated documents; stationary as well as moving forms under variable light intensities; and new-vision enlargements, microscopic images, x-rays, mechanical distortions of reality, direct-light manipulations (photograms), and simultaneous projections, of which photomontage is a preliminary stage.«[2]

In 1928 a thematic photography exhibition called »Pressa« opened in Cologne, and in the same year Walter Dexel organized an exhibition of the work of eight photographers in »Neue Wege der Photographie« (New Paths in Photography) at the Kunstverein in Jena. Subject matter and intended use were the criteria governing the ways the photographs were hung. Portraits, nature, film stills, photomontage, photograms, advertising, and aerial and scientific photography were all represented. The exhibition gave the public a chance to view a wide selection of documentary and scientific photographs as well as examples of the new vision. In the Jena exhibition the needle-sharp and geometrically composed work of Albert Renger-Patzsch, for example, was shown to demonstrate the creative possibilities of the medium's special qualities. »Such photos unlock a whole new world, previously invisible to the eye.«[3] Also included in this exhibit were photographs by László and Lucia Moholy, Walter Peterhans, and Umbo.

The 1928 Jena show truly marked the beginning of a wider acceptance not only of the new vision but also of new concepts in the art of *exhibiting.* Creative photographic works were shown alongside photographs used for industrial, technological, and scientific purposes. Thus, industrial and advertising photographs took on a less functional aspect when seen within the context of formalism as an aesthetic concern for its own sake.

While the Jena exhibition continued, in Stuttgart the organizers of »Film und Foto«, the next big show, were busy with their historically trend-setting project. »Fifo« was meant to show the relationships between photographs in art, advertising, and journalism. Moholy set up an introductory gallery. All visitors passed first through this room, which oriented them to historical developments in photography. Moholy also had a one-person exhibition at »Fifo« that included ninety-seven photographs, photograms, and photo-

sculptures. It is instructive to note that the catalog of this exhibition listed specific photographs as being by Moholy and other new-vision photographers rather than by category—an indication of the new status they were beginning to enjoy. »Film und Foto« was the first international exhibition in which the work of new-vision photographers *as such* was shown. Their work was displayed in the form of posters, printed material, and advertising designs, and each piece was hung as a separate picture. This exhibition gave these innovators a marked degree of legitimacy and a more general level of appreciation than they had previously enjoyed.

The Deutscher Werkbund was the group that organized the »Fifo« exhibition. The primary interest of the Werkbund was in bridging the gap between inventor, producer, and consumer.

To help bring this about, after World War I the Deutscher Werkbund supported a new magazine, *Die Form.* In 1926 an extensive review of Frankfurt's »Deutsche Photographische Ausstellung« appeared in this publication. The reviewer, Eugen Claassen, praised the portraits of Hugo Erfurth and the photographs of sculptures by Walter Hegas. Claassen, however, criticized the dependence of many creative photographers on »painters' schools« and deplored the subservience to clients' control of aesthetic matters in advertising photography. He wrote: »The modern photograph is sociologically and culturally the ersatz art of the bourgeoisie, who are forced to enjoy their aristocratic tastes in a rational form, economically, technically, and intellectually.«[4]

Die Form also published an early discussion of advertising and its relationship to industrial society. In *Typography and Photography* Jan Tschichold wrote about the growing need for creative photography and described the achievements of such foreign photographers as Paul Outerbridge, George Hoyningen-Huene, Baron de Meyer, and Ralph Steiner.

In 1928 books began to appear in which new-vision photographs were reproduced, further spreading the ideas that were developing in

Germany. Among the books that grew out of »Fifo« was Werner Graeff's *Es kommt der neue Fotograf (Here Comes the New Photographer),* which cataloged the direction taken by the new movement in photography. Reproduced were very unorthodox photographs by Oscar and Alice Lex-Nerlinger, Umbo and Andreas, and Lux Feininger.

Ute Eskildsen has stated well the aims of the new-vision photographers:

> The abstracted visual language of the new photographers was based on a structural view of reality, in which the clearly photographic nature of the process was emphasized. According to the formal qualities of a given object, the most favorable angle of representation was sought, utilizing photographic techniques. The photographers of this new objectivity attempted to present known objects as unknown by a variety of optical and chemical means. This encouraged the use of photographs to represent objects in a symbolic manner, which influenced the advertising industry.[5]

In addition to Moholy's often stated ideas about the medium's possibilities for expression, Albert Renger-Patzsch's views, offered at the same period, must be considered. Renger-Patzsch stressed that an object should be photographed from its most favorable structural perspective, paying attention to photography's ability to record the process of creation or fabrication with great clarity. Moholy, on the other hand, saw the medium as light, and the camera as the instrument that could use that light to create images for many purposes. He was a strong advocate of experimentation and felt that photography, because of its technological basis, was especially suited for expressing the spirit of the 20th century. In 1925, which it is interesting to note was the same year that G.F. Hartlaub, the director of the Mannheim *Kunsthalle,* opened the seminal

painting exhibition, »Neue Sachlichkeit«, Moholy published his book *Malerei, Fotografie, Film* in the Bauhaus series. In a chapter of this book, entitled »The Future of the Photographic Process«, Moholy expressed an almost euphoric belief in »optical« possibilities:

> When the true qualities of photography are recognized, the process of representation by mechanical means will be brought to a level of perfection never before attained. (Modern illustrated magazines are still lagging behind, considering their enormous potential!) Thought must be given to what they could and must achieve in the field of education and culture.[6]

The photography section of Moholy's book was a picture show of images that only occasionally referred to the subject in front of the camera. For example, a caption under the photo read: »What was once thought to be distortion is now an amazing experience, a challenge to reevaluate the way we see. It can be viewed from an angle. It always presents a different view.«[7] This book had a marked influence on the »new designers« as well as on photographers. To better understand what was happening in Germany, Moholy's book must be seen in connection with Graeff's *Es kommt der neue Fotograf,* in which he likewise, in words and pictures, declared all previously accepted photographic rules to be null and void.

The »new photography« was discussed by both Renger-Patzsch and Moholy in the yearbook *Das deutsche Lichtbild* (no. 1, 1927). They agreed that photography was an autonomous branch of art, with its own unique and formal qualities. Moholy placed photography within the field of visual art, according it a special place because of its sensitivity to light, and proclaimed his interest in it as a new image-making system. Renger-Patzsch emphasized the camera's ability to record reality even beyond what we normally observe. He said:

The secret of a good photograph—which like a work of art may possess aesthetic qualities—is its realism. . . . Let us therefore leave art to artists and endeavor to create photography that will last because of its photographic quality, because its uniquely photographic property hasn't been borrowed from another art.[8]

Serious criticism dealing with the aims of objective photography began to appear in the mid-20s in well regarded art and photography magazines. An example would be Willi Warstat's 1929 insightful review of the Moholy book *Malerei, Fotografie, Film.* In 1929 Franz Roh's and Jan Tschichold's book *Foto Auge/Œil et Photo/ Photo Eye* was published. Most of the photographs reproduced had been included in the »Film und Foto« exhibition. In his essay, Roh defined a photographic aesthetic that emphasized the independent character of the medium, thus further establishing photography as a serious means of expression.

In the late 1920s a number of magazines began to publish separate sections featuring the »new photography.« The German editors selected arresting photographs that were usually unrelated to each other and reproduced them with merely a title and at times the photographer's name. These pictures were presented as one might see them in an exhibition and became a showcase for examples of the new vision as well as commercial photography that incorporated these new aesthetic dimensions.

The most interesting of these was *Der Querschnitt (The Profile)* in which photographs with completely different meanings—which added up to a third effect that was often humorous or referred to current life-styles—were frequently reproduced next to each other. Umbo, Sander, Salomon, Hajek-Halke, and Sasha Stone, among others, supplied photographs for this lively periodical.

Magazines and yearbooks increasingly reproduced new-vision photographs, but exhibitions were still a very important means of acquainting the public with the achievements of the avantgarde photographers.

Until Hitler came into prominence in 1922, large, rather freewheeling photography exhibitions continued to be held almost every year. They served to expand awareness of the new vision, and they encouraged advertisers to utilize the talents of those photographers who worked in this fashion. In 1930 the exhibition »Das Lichtbild« (The Photograph) opened in Munich and included portions of »Film und Foto«. This was an important exhibition because German photographers not seen in »Film und Foto« were included, such as Hein Gorny, Lotte Jacobi, Edmund Kesting, and August Sander. »Das Lichtbild« was followed in 1931 by an exhibition of the same name in Essen's Museum Folkwang. Originated by Max Burchartz and Kurt Wilhelm-Kaestner, it placed emphasis on new photographic techniques, many of which were demonstrated at the exhibition. Wilhelm-Kaestner wrote of the aims of the exhibition in *Die Wochenschau:* »The ideal value of photography is primarily to teach our eyes—clouded by learning and knowledge—to see and recognize our environment and to increase our perceptive capabilities.«[9]

The new vision was certainly not solely the invention of Moholy and Renger-Patzsch—a viewpoint that might be arrived at by reading the above brief history of German photographic exhibitions. It is true that with intelligence and insight these two men awakened people to photography's potential for re-seeing what advanced technology meant to the world on one hand, and nature's relationship to humankind on the other. It is equally true that a number of other photographers with imagination and courage also made substantial contributions to the development of this avantgarde movement.

It is not surprising that Moholy's wife, Lucia, a major photographer in her own right, was among those who freed creative photography from the grip of the amateur pictorialists and helped to create a new visual language.

She was a very active collaborator in Moholy's investigations of photography, and, because he was not very proficient in German, she helped him with his writing.

LUCIA MOHOLY, Czech by birth, studied philosophy and art history before she met Moholy in Berlin in 1920, and married him the following year. She learned developing and printing techniques soon after they were married so that she could do darkroom work. Lucia copied the photograms she and Moholy made with glass-plate negatives so that publication and exhibition prints could be made in large sizes–the original prints were single, relatively small, unique images and were subject to fading, having often been made on printout paper or postcard stock. We are very grateful today for Lucia Moholy's work in this area, because few of the original photograms they made have survived from those early years in Germany. The largest copies of Moholy's photograms were not, however, made by Lucia; the copies she printed never exceeded 18 x 24 cm. When she left Germany in 1933, over five hundred negatives remained. Other people then seem to have made prints from her negatives. While she has never again seen the negatives of her husband's photographs or his photograms, she was able to retrieve a number of her own negatives of people and architecture.

In addition to this collaboration, Lucia Moholy did independent work. Every day she saw the buildings of the Bauhaus in Dessau, for her husband was a master teacher there. She photographed these new buildings in direct response to the sense of dynamism the structures evoked. Shooting from above or below created slanted elements against the sky and focused attention on the spare, repeated, and interlocked elements that were new as architectural forms.

Walter Gropius, who designed the major Bauhaus buildings, did not like Lucia Moholy's photographs of his structures. He preferred straightforward documents made at ground level rather than her freewheeling interpretations of his work. She, however, was interested in conveying the spiritual nature of the structures, not just in documenting them. By using the lens's capacity for creating unusual views of buildings, she was able to imbue her photographs with something of the conceptual energy that went into their evolution. She understood well that a diagonal form or line that recedes in a picture conveys a feeling of movement, even in a solidly planted concrete building. Like ships at the dock and airplanes on the ground, the complex of Bauhaus buildings seems to have the capacity for movement even though they are quite still. This as well as the marvelous juxtaposition of nature's design–in the form of trees–and man's ingenious solution to the problems of structure were also conveyed in her photographs.

A second and most impressive facet of her work was her portraiture. Many of her subjects were artists, architects, and photographers who were more susceptible to new interpretations of themselves than most people. She took full advantage of this and often moved in close to the faces of her subjects. In so doing she recorded eyes, noses, and lips as geometric shapes uniquely combined to make up the identifying characteristics by which we recognize people. Her approach was in keeping with the lively new epoch and its delight in purely formal concerns, coupled with the material reality only the photograph could convey. That her portraits also evoke some of the personality of her subjects is significant and speaks of her insights and warmth as a person.

In 1934 Lucia Moholy went to London, where she taught photography and aesthetics and wrote the respected history *A Hundred Years of Photography, 1839-1939.* She now lives in Zurich.

CHRISTIAN SCHAD was one of the German artists who showed interest in the processes of photographic abstraction even before Moholy started his investigations into the creative possibilities of this medium. At the time he was not considered to be among the new-vision photographers because of his limited involvement with the medium. He must be included in any history of the period, however, because of his very early use of photographic means to create symbolic imagery.

Part of his aim was to break their connection with their everyday functions. In 1918 Schad made some dada »collages« of printed tickets and other graphic items and then contact-printed them on photosensitive paper so that their negative aspect was recorded. These little »Schadographs,« as Tristan Tzara called them, were thought of as a means of changing discarded printed items into objects possessing unpredictable qualities—an interpretation consistent with his aims in associating with the dada movement. Moholy could have seen a reproduction of Schad's imagery made in this fashion that was included in the seventh issue of *Dada* (»Dadaphone,« March 1920). Although under Schad's influence he does not seem to have taken up the photogram process, as Moholy called it, he was inspired by Man Ray's experiments in a similar direction. Schad is still active as a Neue Sachlichkeit painter and in recent years has again made more Schadographs.

Moving from 1919 to 1930, we encounter GYORGY KEPES, a Hungarian and one of Moholy's most gifted followers in Berlin. Since 1937 he has lived in the United States, where he is known as a photographer, painter, collagemaker, and teacher. Earlier in his career, in Berlin, he became an explorer of new vistas and viewpoints with the camera.

Kepes first studied painting at the Academy of Fine Arts in Budapest, but by 1929 he was working in motion pictures. From Budapest he went to Berlin in 1930 at Moholy's invitation. During the next five years he experimented with both motion and still photography. He made

dramatic use of low camera positions and the late-afternoon rays of the sun as it cast long shadows and silhouetted forms when the lens was pointed toward the light. This was an old pictorialist practice, but Kepes chose unromantic subjects—such as Berlin's crowded streets—to evoke a looming, aggressive presence in his pictures. As might be expected from a photographer who was a friend of Moholy, Kepes also took some very design-oriented photographs of street intersections from high above them. In these he succeeded in flattening out the sense of space to the point that the elements became almost low and relieflike in appearance.

In 1936 Kepes joined Moholy in London and then followed him to Chicago, where in 1937 Kepes became the head of the light department—which included photography—at the New Bauhaus. In 1945 he joined the faculty of the Massachusetts Institute of Technology and introduced visual-design courses into the curriculum of the School of Architecture. While still active as a photographer and painter, he has retired as a teacher and lives in Cambridge, Massachusetts.

HANS RICHTER, another friend of Moholy, was a major innovative filmmaker in Germany who also became involved with the dadaists in the early 1920s. On at least one occasion Richter had printed 1 1/4-x-1 1/2-inch prints from a series of frames taken with a movie camera, such as the ones of the three floating derby hats. This sequence from his 1928 film, *Vormittagsspuk (Ghosts Before Breakfast),* inevitably recalls René Magritte's surreal imagery. A type of lyricism is evoked that is unusual for Germany but very much in line with various manifestations of surrealism in France during the early, vital years of the movement's success.

It has often been overlooked that WALTER PETERHANS taught the only photography courses offered at the Bauhaus. As the son of the director of the Zeiss-Ikon Company, he was naturally given a camera at an early age. He soon became well-acquainted with the full range of photographic techniques. After service in the German army during World War I, he studied mathematics, philosophy, and art history at Göttingen University. His formal training in photography and art took place at the Staatliche Akademie für Graphische Künste und Buchgewerbe (Academy for Graphic Arts) in Leipzig. There he learned etching, photoreproduction techniques, and photography. From 1929 to 1932 he taught as a master at the Bauhaus in Dessau, where he established the department of photography. In 1932, under the direction of Mies van der Rohe, the Bauhaus relocated in Berlin, and a revised curriculum was developed at the Reimann-Häring-Schule. Peterhans was responsible for those students who elected in their second stage to concentrate on photography. He gave them a practical, rigidly disciplined, technical, and scientific photography background with an emphasis on straightforward mastery of the translation of colors into black and white. He then directed the students to move from technical experimentation toward mastery of the techniques of advertising and reporting.

Unlike so many other German photographers, Peterhans did not use unusual perspectives or forms as a means of attracting attention to his own work. In the spare Bauhaus surroundings, Peterhans saw the camera as a straightforward recording instrument, yet on occasion he made oddly haunting pictures in which space was not clearly defined. For example, a flower blossom was made to suggest the odd grace and beauty of elegiac poetry. His pictures seem to take on qualities we associate with the brilliant light of the desert or life by the sea. They usually grew, however, out of an interest in recording the textural nature of high-quality manufactured goods and arranging forms in a coherent fashion.

Today we see that his instinct vied with his intellect, for he was the rare exception among those at the Bauhaus who saw everything in terms of geometry. Surrealism, the most talked-about new art movement in the 1930s, must be

seen as having provided a background for his still-life pictures, which are most highly thought of today.

Peterhans went to Chicago in 1939 and from then until 1960 taught visual awareness and art history classes in the department of architecture at the Institute of Design. He died in Germany in 1960 on a return trip to his homeland.

Like Peterhans, ARVID GUTSCHOW began photography as an amateur while he was a schoolboy. To help earn his living, he worked as a commercial photographer after he left high school and began to study law. The success of his photographs led to assignments for prominent magazines. In 1930 his book *See, Sand, Sonne* was published and was recognized as reflecting an important break with conventional photographic treatment of landscapes. His pictures allowed nature to reveal the very energy and mystery of the act of creation and established a feeling of oneness with the origins of humankind. He did this in unsentimental terms, which had great appeal for those who were seeking philosophical symbols for contemporary discoveries by anthropologists and other scientists probing for answers to humankind's roots. Gutschow continued his involvement with photography while carrying out his duties as a civil servant in Hamburg.

Related, both in terms of content and philosophy, to Gutschow's work were the photographs of ALFRED EHRHARDT.

To our eyes, conditioned to viewing paintings that are involved with imagery parallel to the picture's plane or that have forms that seem to shift toward deep, almost infinite space, the photographs that Ehrhardt made of sandy shallows by the Baltic Sea are especially exciting.

The spiritual stimuli of nature was deeply rooted in German philosophy. Ehrhardt was seeking to evoke the essence of nature when he reduced his subjects, such as the sand flats and shells, to their rudimentary shapes in order to

I. Alfred Ehrhardt, Dunes – Kurische Nehrung, 1936

convey the idea that the multiplicity of forms they assumed grew out of similar patterns of growth and time. The concepts he was dealing with were old, but his photographs were a departure from tradition–considering the high level of artistic achievement: His use of middle-gray tones, simplified forms, and ambiguous effects of space are unique in the photography of the 1930s. In Germany there was great interest in sand, sea, and sun and what they symbolized as manifestations of nature, but most photographers who took the sand and shoreline as subjects treated them more literally than did Ehrhardt, giving emphasis to shadows and conventional perspective. Ehrhardt used a low camera position to cause the sand to occupy the major part of the foreground and gave little space to the sky in his compositions. In at least one instance he tilted his camera in a way that caused the horizon to cut diagonally across one corner of a picture–a very daring break with tradition. Ehrhardt's sandscapes focus on tone and pattern rather than a specific scene in nature. This, plus the scaleless and uninterrupted patterns made by the sea-washed sand, recall early pictures of the moon before the landing of the astronauts.

In short, Ehrhardt photographed the sands of the seacoast with his camera firmly anchored to the earth, even though the results may seem extraterrestrial to us.

ROBERT PETSCHOW, an engineer turned balloonist, created landscapes as enigmatic as Ehrhardt's. Petschow taught himself photography to record the marvelous vistas he saw below him while silently floating over the German countryside. He was active during World War I in lighter-than-air crafts and continued to be a flyer in the 1920s and 1930s. His photographs recall abstract paintings–flat and patterned. The camera's eye sees the world in a flatter aspect than do human eyes. For this reason a very objective photograph that does not contain a foreground object as a measure of the distance between near and far appears to be a flat plane with only trees or houses to serve as relief elements. Petschow's information-filled photographs test our perceptions and charm us with the delightful puzzles they present for us to solve.

Moholy would have probably also liked to be a balloonist but was busy teaching–having been appointed a Bauhaus master in 1923 to supervise the foundation course. He did not teach photography as a specific subject but encouraged his students by exhortation and example to try out all aspects of the medium as part of their studies of the properties of light. We find his influence reflected in the work of most 1920s avant-garde photographers. It can be seen most clearly in Andreas Feininger's work, even though Moholy was not actually his teacher.

ANDREAS FEININGER was the son of the artist Lyonel Feininger, a master at the Bauhaus. Born in France, he was educated at the Bauhaus. Between 1929 and 1933 he experimented with many aspects of photography while living and studying in Dessau and Paris. In 1933 he moved to Sweden and became a professional photographer specializing in pictures of architecture, ships, machines, and details of biological specimens. Feininger was a true explorer. Taking his cue from Moholy, he tried all kinds of manipulation. He used several negatives printed together to give the effect of bas-relief. He tried negative prints and also reticulated his negatives to enlarge the grains of silver so that the grains became an overall design element. In 1936 he moved to New York City, where he carried out a wide range of assignments for *Life* magazine and produced a number of books of his photographs. He still lives in New York part of every year.

Moholy's influence can also be seen in the pictures of the innovative photographer WERNER DAVID FEIST, a Bauhaus student in 1928-1929, but it was Peterhans who taught him the techniques of photography. Moholy had only an indirect influence on his use of the medium. Both Feist and Lux Feininger, Andreas's brother, knew Moholy only on a casual social basis, for he left the Bauhaus in 1928 and moved to Berlin. Lux Feininger and Feist, in 1928-1929, were both associated with Bauhaus stage performances—which may explain their use of dramatic distortions. Feist's tightly framed picture of the sound arm of a gramophone was intentionally taken so close to the camera that a kind of lens distortion took place, giving the forms a monumental character.

His picture of Milon Harms, a fellow student in graphic design, was, as Feist recalls, made to emphasize this northern German's Adam's apple, the rough texture of his skin, and his dense head of hair, and to indicate that he derived great pleasure from chain-smoking. Feist also tried sandwiched negatives and other abstracting devices to enliven his imagery. He continued his interest in photography but became a graphic designer—first in Germany and then in Canada. He now lives in Montreal.

Moholy worked in England for a year, and Lucia Moholy worked there for many years, but few other photographers who were members of the German avant-garde made Great Britain their home after Hitler came to power. W. M. HEINZ LOEW, who was a student at the Bauhaus from 1926 to 1930, is an exception. In Germany in the late 1920s he made some very successful images that convey the discord and vibrancy of

the decade. With skill and imagination he combined a photograph of a man playing drums with a phonograph turntable and playing arm. Such juxtapositions recall Edmund Kesting's use of similar techniques and predate Hajek-Halke's pictures. A wide range of associations were metaphorically evoked by incorporating within a single frame diversely scaled and lighted elements that crystalized into a symbol of the photographer's responses to what was going on around him or her. Loew continued his career after World War II in England, where he lives in semiretirement.

LUX FEININGER, in addition to his interest in the theater, was a member of the Bauhaus dance band in Dessau. His photographs of members of the band were notable for their exaggerations. Shooting up at a saxophonist and a banjo player conveyed some of the brash quality of their jazz, then so very popular in Germany. In other instances he used high and low camera positions to dramatize, by lens distortion, pictures of people. In one striking image he utilized the camera's one-eye characteristic of merging near and far to catch two athletes seemingly jumping over the Bauhaus. His arresting photograph of Clemens Roeseler, a Bauhaus-trained painter and self-taught musician, was taken in early 1928 before Feininger began to use an enlarger regularly. It was carefully composed within the

II. Werner David Feist, Portrait Milon Harms, 1929

III. Lux Feininger, »The Jump over the Bauhaus«, ca. 1928

frame, as were all of his early photographs. Later, during his short career as a photographer, he relied more on the possibility of composing in the darkroom on his enlarger's paper holder. A highly spirited young man, Lux Feininger refused to confine himself to conventional uses of the camera. His sophisticated snapshots reverberate with a zest for life and a playfulness. Unfortunately for photography, after his youthful period of experimentation with the camera, he devoted his energies to painting. He is now retired and lives in Cambridge, Massachusetts.

While the Bauhaus was perhaps the best-known school of design, other innovative schools did exist. At one of these schools HANS FINSLER taught one of the few classes in Germany that competed with Peterhans's courses of instruction at the Bauhaus and Max Burchartz's Folkwang classes in Essen. Like Peterhans and Burchartz, Finsler taught basic photography with full knowledge of the new vision. Crisp details, strong designs, and close-ups of manufactured products arranged with great attention to geometric repetition of forms were almost always characteristic of his work. Swiss born, Finsler first studied architecture in Munich, where he became acquainted with modern art. Most of the photographers of the period served in the various armies during World War I. Being from a neutral country, however, Finsler studied art history with the great

IV. Werner Rohde, »Haut den Lukas«-Figure, 1931

V. Alice Lex-Nerlinger, from: »Es kommt der neue Fotograf!«

scholar Heinrich Wölfflin during the war years. The analytical methods taught by Wölfflin plus the disciplined training Finsler received as a student of architecture influenced his later development as a photographer. In 1922 he was appointed librarian and taught art history at the Werkstätten Burg Giebichenstein (School of Arts and Crafts) in Halle, Germany. He next became an instructor of photography there. His own photographs and those of his students attracted the attention of companies wishing to publish strikingly illustrated catalogs of their products and advertising agencies serving imaginative clients who were moving ahead in manufacturing and marketing. There were not many photographers in the 1920s and early 1930s who could produce pictures with the modern look. As a consequence Finsler was kept very busy with both commercial work and teaching.

Before World War II he returned to his native Zurich and taught some of the best-known post-World War II Swiss photographers, including Werner Bischof, Emil Schulthess, and René Burri. He died in Zurich in 1972, a year after his major book, *My Way to Photography,* was published.

WERNER ROHDE's father did paintings on glass. This humble craft inspired his son to study art. In 1925 he began his art career by attending Professor E. Haas's painting classes at the Werkstätten Burg Giebichenstein, the school in Halle where Hans Finsler taught photography. There Rohde was introduced to the process of photomontage, and in 1927 he began to make his own photographs. He worked in Paris the following years, and in 1930 he returned to Bremen, where he made his living as a photographer while interning as a painter. In Halle he had met Moholy, and in Paris, Paul Citroen, both of whose work influenced his photography.

HERBERT BAYER was influenced by Moholy and in turn seemed to have influenced Moholy. Because he was born in Austria, he was called up to serve in the Austrian-Hungarian Army during World War I. He then became an apprentice in architecture for a year in Linz under Georg Schmidthammer. In 1920 he moved to Darmstadt, Germany, to assist the architect Emanuel Margold in graphic design. During the years 1921-1923 he was a student at the Bauhaus in Weimar and became closely associated with Moholy. As there were no jobs available, he worked as a house painter in 1923 and 1924. The next year he was appointed a master at the Bauhaus, teaching typography and advertising layout. In 1925 he moved to Berlin where he became much interested in photography while continuing to do graphic and exhibition design. As a graphic designer he often made use of photomontages. Some of his imagery was based on photographs he found, while he photographed other parts to fit his concept of what was needed in a particular collage. Jan van der Marck has said of Bayer's best-known collage, Self-Portrait, 1932/1935, »The handsome youth and the conjunction of marble and flesh are straight from the Surrealist vocabulary, the beauty of classical, especially Greek, sculpture was much in Bayer's mind from 1930 until 1938.«[10] During 1936 Bayer fabricated a number of unconventional still-life scenes specifically to be photographed.

Bayer was one of the first designers to use photographs instead of drawings or paintings in posters. He felt that photographs would be more effective than the traditional types of illustration, because the camera is not subjective and pictures made with it would show objects as they actually are rather than as imagined.

In some of his »Fotoplastiken« he set up objects in his studio using strings to prop them up. The compositions were then photographed. Afterward he would airbrush out the supporting strings and sometimes add tiny clouds. The retouched photographs were then photographed for reproduction and exhibition. These images incorporated a sense of deep, almost infinite space. They were derived from childhood memories of alpine peasant life—an environment of farm implements, barn doors, animal skeletal remains, and mountain vistas. In some instances the forms are bonelike, which cause his photographs to recall the work of Dali. Bayer dealt with space in plastic rather than linear terms, as had Moholy in his collages. The iconography of Bayer's work was, however, more related to the rigors of geometry than to the uncertain qualities of the dream state.

In 1938 Bayer moved to New York and designed the Museum of Modern Art's historic exhibition, Bauhaus 1919-1928; he also edited its catalog. He moved to Aspen, Colorado, in 1946 to act as consultant and architect for the Aspen Institute for Humanistic Studies. In 1975, for reasons of health, he moved to Montecito, California, where he now lives.

IRENE BAYER, Herbert Bayer's first wife, was born in Chicago but was taken to Europe when she was a child. She finished high school in Hungary and in 1920 left for Berlin. There she studied commercial art for a year and a half. In 1923 she went to Weimar to see the great Bauhaus exhibition. This experience changed her direction, and she decided to educate herself in the fine arts. She moved to Paris where she met Léger and Picasso and attended lectures at the Sorbonne. In late 1924 she returned to Weimar, where she met Herbert Bayer. They were married in 1925, and in the following year they moved to Dessau. She then decided to learn photography in order to assist her husband in his work. After learning the techniques of photography at the Leipzig Academy, she began working with Herbert on his commercial art designs.

Her own photographs were often of people. Some of them were treated as subjects for interpretive purposes, while others served as formal motifs. In the former, the faces were full framed to get the maximum effect of the individual's features. When she used the human form as a motif, she would sometimes offset the head and take the picture from above. This created a feeling as if she had just barely caught the person as he or she moved out of camera range.

During World War II she returned to the United States. When hostilities ended, she went back to Europe to serve as a translator and chief of the American photo section in Munich. In 1947 she came back to the United States. She is now retired and lives in Santa Monica, California.

OSCAR and ALICE NERLINGER are the third husband and wife team of photographers whose work is important in this period. Oscar Nerlinger spent his youth in Strasbourg but came to Berlin to study art at the Kunstgewerbemuseum. There he met Alice Lex and married her in 1918. Both artists used photomontage and photogram techniques. This permitted them to combine very different kinds and sizes of imagery to create flat shapes that interacted graphically. Alice also used an amalgam of two images to give form to an idea broader than could be conveyed by a single photograph. Her single-image pictures express powerful emotions by separating parts of the body, such as tightly gripped hands.

Oscar became involved with the worker's movement and contributed photogram illustrations to the movement's press. The photograms created a context for photographic elements without making them specific in connotation. That is to say, the nature of the photogram abstracts information but the essential nature of forms is retained, making his images quite posterlike and easily read in conjunction with text. He also explored the graphic possibilities of bold, negative prints.

Because of their involvement with politics and avant-garde art, the Nerlingers were not permitted to carry on their work in Germany after Hitler came to power. Alice left for Italy and continued her interest in political and social matters. After World War II she returned to Germany; she died in Berlin. Oscar turned to landscapes as his subject after 1933. After the end of World War II he became a professor of art at the Hochschule

für Bildende Kunst in Berlin, where he died in 1969.

As was the case with the Nerlingers a number of avant-garde photographers working in Germany were not connected with the Bauhaus or the other innovative design schools.

WERNER MANTZ's photographs would seem to link him with the Bauhaus, so related are they in style to the geometry we think of in connection with that school and its philosophies of design. Mantz's development, however, was independent of the Bauhaus.

As a boy living in Cologne, Mantz was a very enthusiastic amateur photographer. Soon after the end of World War I he decided to become a professional photographer and went to Munich to study with Professor Spoerl at the Bayerische Staatslehranstalt für Fotografie (Bavarian State Academy for Photography) until 1921. Upon completing his studies, he returned to Cologne and set up a studio. One of his early clients was an architect working in the new, simplified style. The photographs he did were a success, and Mantz was recommended to other architects. Mantz developed an understanding of the new movement in architecture and learned to convey the special formal qualities of buildings, electrical and plumbing apparatus, and conveyors. His careful selection of existing light situations added a sense of drama to the clearly recorded design of the subjects he was asked to photograph.

Interest in his photographs depends today not upon whether they summed up the merits of an advertiser's product or were pleasing to an architect but upon their ability to hold our attention as pictures of artistic merit. His photographs, aside from serving useful purposes, often upstaged the product or building they were intended to complement. For instance, far outweighing its connection with the products of the Ada cheese factory was Mantz's bold photographic interpretation of the factory, in which he printed together three negatives so skillfully that we initially accept the composite view as a straight-forward print.

In 1932 German architecture was at a standstill due to the political uncertainty of the times. In that year Mantz moved to Maastricht, Holland, where he began specializing in children's portraits. He has remained in Holland ever since. It can now be seen that his pictures of architecture are his most innovative and relevant to the times.

To get beyond mere transcription HEINZ HAJEK-HALKE, who has spent most of his creative years in Berlin, experimented with negative prints, sandwiched negatives, and montages. The results, while in the spirit of Moholy's work, are more romantic than modern. This is due partly to the way in which he used the nude female figure as a recurring and contrasting form and as a symbol. His surrealism is late modern, and like all late manifestations of a vibrant movement there is a manneristic quality to his »dreams« and a somewhat stilted look to his designs. He is one of the few photographers who began his career around 1930 and continued to make strong visual statements in Germany a decade after the ending of World War II. He continues to live in Berlin.

Working in techniques similar to those employed by Hajek-Halke was an early critic of art photography, FRANZ ROH. He called photographers who aspired to create art with a camera »Raphaels without hands«[11] and deplored the photographs that were derived in formal terms from painting and pretended to be drawings or charcoal sketches. Nevertheless, we can now see that many of his photographs, while not related to paintings of conventional subjects, were inspired by the ideas of avant-garde artists. He did not escape the photographic mannerisms of his time that—while he may not have thought so—were often directly borrowed from new design and painting movements such as Art Deco and surrealism. Early in his development Roh made negative prints by sandwiching two negatives and printing them together to interrelate the images of both, evoking a dreamlike form of symbolism related to Freud's ideas, which were under serious discussion in the late 1920s and 1930s.

Germany became increasingly unstable, politically and financially, as the 1920s came to a close. Because of this, in 1929 EWALD HOINKIS left the world of business administration to become a graphic designer and photographer. He had been a serious amateur photographer since 1920 and had received recognition for his work in this field. He took up his new career in his native city of Görlitz but soon moved to Berlin where his posters, designs, and photographs for advertising and his catalog work brought him success. He was a pioneer color photographer in the mid-1930s and often carried out assignments for Ullstein publications. Particular attention was given to formal and structural solutions to design problems, and he combined type with photographs in a fashion that gave his arrangements instant visual impact. Recognizing his skills and imagination, the Meisterschule für Grafik und Buchgewerbe (School for Graphic Design and Bookbinding) appointed him to a teaching position in 1937. He continued to do independent work, but it lacked the spirit of adventuresomeness found in his best early photographs.

WILLY OTTO ZIELKE, whose photographs have much in common with Hoinkis's, came from Lodz in Poland, but he and his family lived in Russia until 1921. As a consequence he first studied railway engineering in Tashkent, Russia, then attended the Bayerische Staatslehranstalt für Fotografie in Munich. His early experience with machinery gave him a respect for precision and order—characteristics of his work with the camera. In the 1930s Zielke became known for his beautifully crafted light-filled compositions.

His restrained photographs, many of which are still-life arrangements, are a far cry from the cool exactitude of Renger-Patzsch's pictures of similar subjects. His work of this nature falls somewhat on the classic side of Herbert Lizt's surreal set pieces, which will be referred to later. In Zielke's photographs there is a feeling of equivocation that probably stems from the relative lateness of his emergence as a new-vision photographer. Revealed by his arrangements of forms was an apprenticeship in modern design that provided him with the ideas for his studies of piles of sheets of window glass, bottles, boxes, and modern accessory items that have a fine and intricate delicacy. His intention was to impart a sense of richness to objects by using subtly contrasting textures. He treated his subjects like jewels enhanced by their settings. In his pictures intervals and proportions were handled with great sensitivity and light as defining agents. His closely focused work expressed an enjoyment of art as a challenge to his skills, and while precise, is unforced and still has a feeling of dynamism. This quality made Zielke's 1935 film on German railroads outstanding.

Most of the photographers who left Germany after Hitler consolidated his hold on the country came to New York City. On the other hand, in 1933 JOHN GUTMANN chose San Francisco as the place to reestablish his life and career. An established avant-garde painter, he had only begun to photograph shortly before leaving Germany. His training as a painter gave him a sense of form that—coupled with perceptions he had gained from looking at published photographers—made him an immediate success as a photojournalist. He received assignments from a German editor and was accepted, on a commission basis, to do work for a photo agency in Berlin when he left for America. His brooding pictures taken in 1933 were visceral responses to how he felt about being forced to leave Germany. In the United States he has fared well as a professor at San Francisco State University, teaching painting and photography.

SASHA STONE came to the United States early in his life. Born in Russia, he was brought up and educated in America in technical drafting for the aircraft industry, then left this field to study art in Paris. It is not clear when he took up photography, but by the early 1930s he had a studio in Berlin. He then moved to Brussels. He had as his clients prominent industrial companies and famous architects, including Erich Mendelsohn.

Stone had a sure, exacting eye for creating unusual arrangements of objects that extolled the virtues of his clients' products. His technical and artistic background had given him an awareness of how, through the use of light and placement, to convey the attractive qualities of any form. Stone's strength was in the heightened intensity he was able to evoke from such ordinary subjects as shoes. Shoes are familiar to us all in their new and worn states, but Stone made symbols of them simply by the way he treated them photographically. Such disarming subjects touch us, for they open our eyes to shared experiences.

Like that of Zielke and Finsler, Stone's work was borderline when considered as avant-garde but serves well to clarify our perceptions of what was new during the period 1919 to 1939.

A person whose work was more art-oriented than Stone's was EDMUND KESTING. He shared the attitude of the most inventive photographers of the period and generated excitement by exploiting, like Seidenstücker, the camera's eye for caught moments and new viewpoints. Kesting studied painting for a number of years before turning to photography. Born in Dresden, he attended the academy of art there from 1911 to 1916. War service from 1916 to 1918 interrupted his training. Upon his return to Dresden and the academy, he studied briefly with Richard Müller and Otto Gussmann. In 1919 he founded the art school Der Weg in Dresden and became connected with Der Sturm circle and its founder, Herwarth Walden. From painting he turned to work in collage and photography, frequently employing double exposures. His was a high level of expressionism coupled with knowledge of cubism and surrealism. It is interesting to note that preceding World War I, in Kesting's native city, the young artists Erich Heckel, Karl Schmidt-

Rottluff, and Max Pechstein founded Die Brücke, which broke drastically with German art-history traditions of the times. Kesting was an inheritor of this spirit of rebellion.

One of Kesting's finest pictures was made in 1927. It was a closely cropped view of his wife in a car—a view fragmented by the frame of the car's window, out of which we see a typical German house with a peaked roof. A reflection of another house on the glass windscreen echoes this image. From a formal standpoint the reflections are flat to the plane of the picture and give emphasis to the diagonal dashboard of the car. The big, carefully calculated vertical divisions of the picture, outlined by the frames of the window and support of the windshield, provide openings in which are found various visual vignettes. One contains, in profile, a third of a person's face; in another, the driver's hand, which is cut through by the reflection, giving it a striking near/far feeling. Another vignette frames sharply defined portions of the steering wheel and of the clamps that hold down what was probably a canvas top. Though done over fifty years ago, this Horch advertisement is a strikingly contemporary picture both in terms of its concept as well as its formal qualities.

Another strikingly new image, a close-up of a woman's face, caught a fleeting expression of amusement just as the corners of her mouth lifted and her mood changed. This picture makes us aware of the expressive possibilities of a discerning eye and a ready camera when it comes to dealing merely with portions of a person's body to evoke an emotional response. Kesting's use of a dramatic, elongated shadow from a second negative in a self-portrait was also innovative. His subtle use of partial solarization in a picture of a young woman's face, across which falls a part negative, part positive shadow of the blossom of a flower, divorces the image from the subject recorded by the camera. His larger-than-life photographs of faces combined with a few notes from nature, such as flowers, convey a feeling of a flat pattern and reveal the formal structure of the human face. In these pictures, like those of Aenne Biermann and Raoul Hausmann, the face is a motif seen from an unaccustomed angle—which heightens the sense of immediacy.

After Hitler took over in Germany in 1933, a spiritual malaise set in. First there was a drift toward anti-intellectualism and against experimentation in the arts. A rigid code was established that made innovation almost impossible. Due to his association with the avant-garde movement, Kesting was not allowed to exhibit or work as an artist. In 1955 he became a professor at the Deutsche Hochschule für Filmkunst in Dresden, but the innovative quality of his work had slackened, and he lost the ability to command attention.

Kesting's portraits and double exposures, as well as his pictures evoking a deep sense of space, were analogous in some ways to the close-ups and tilted angles used in such popular films as *The Cabinet of Dr. Caligari* and *The Blue Angel.* It was, however, the probing portraits of HELMAR LERSKI that were most cinematic. Lerski tried to penetrate the mask people held up to the public. His menacing, multilighted pictures of faces only rarely achieve this goal, but they certainly convey the pulse of life in Berlin—that city of dash and daring in films, theater, and in journals such as *Der Sturm.* They evoke the Berlin of Bertolt Brecht, Kurt Weill, George Grosz, and Lotte Lenya more than any other still photographs. When viewing Lerski's pictures, one thinks of the staccato rhythms of *Die Dreigroschenoper* or the bizarrely lighted close-ups of Peter Lorre in *M.*

Lerski had a varied career. In 1893, at the age of 22, he came to America from Zurich. For a number of years he was an actor in New York and then joined a company that played in Chicago and Milwaukee. In 1911 he first turned to photography. This was natural, for his wife was a photographer. While talking to some fellow actors in her studio in Milwaukee, he decided to use his knowledge of light and staging to do some photography himself.

After these first experiments he became increasingly involved with a new type of portraiture that used unusual placement of shadows, such as one might find in eerie stage settings where the lighting came from below.

In 1912 one of Europe's leading portraitists, the Hamburg-based Rudolph Dührkoop, came to St. Louis to demonstrate his dramatic techniques. Lerski showed Dührkoop his pictures and received enthusiastic encouragement. As a result Lerski gave up the stage for photography. He next went to Austin, where he taught photography and German at the University of Texas. He moved to Berlin the following year. There he became a cameraman at the UFA (Universum-Film-Aktiengesellschaft) studio for fourteen years. He managed the camera for films by Paul Leni and Berthold Viertel. With the advent of sound in 1929, he returned to still photography. In all of his still portraits he filled the entire frame with his subject's head, then lighted the face with mirrors— sometimes using as many as sixteen. Once he had mastered this technique, he always used daylight, with the sun placed behind his subject's head. Because the sun was always at the back of his model, he had complete control as he manipulated the mirrors to cast shadows and create highlights wherever he wanted.

In the early 1930s Lerski left Germany for Palestine, where in 1937 and 1938 he produced »Verwandlung durch Licht« (»Transformation Through Light«). This study of one hundred seventy-five portraits was the culmination of his career as a still photographer. In Palestine, Lerski again became a motion-picture cameraman for documentary films. In 1948 he returned to Zurich, where he died in 1956.

A photographer whose work is somewhat related in appearance to Lerski's studies of people's faces was ERICH RETZLAFF. In 1930 his close-ups of old people were published in *Das Antlitz des Alters,* and at about the same time *Menschen am Werk* appeared. The very strong photographs included in these publications were less self-conscious than Lerski's somewhat similar portraits. After creating the dramatic close-ups, Retzlaff, like August Sander, turned to landscapes, which were less controversial than portraits that had social overtones. Retzlaff was an early color photographer and received recognition for this type of work around 1940. His color landscapes were quite romantic, which made them popular during the period of the Third Reich.

RAOUL HAUSMANN, like Kesting and Aenne Biermann, made larger-than-life photographs that cause us to become ultraconscious of the shape of parts of the face. Hausmann was born in Vienna, where his father was an artist. In 1918, as an early dada poet and editor of a dada journal in Berlin, young Hausmann became involved with art. A friend of Moholy during the early 1920s, he is best known for his use of pieces of photographs in collages of text and images that deal with social disruption and the turbulent years immediately following World War I. He later made some impressive, straight photographs. During the period 1927 to 1931 he juxtaposed snippets of photographs to produce nonpolitical and nonmodified photographs that seem to have been taken from unusual viewpoints. He had a keen eye for the primal reality of people and things from the everyday world, out of which he created a wealth of fresh pictorial ideas. Some of his ideas were unique; others paralleled what his fellow artists were doing in the 1930s with the newly discovered possibilities of camera-vision. Among his close-ups of flowers, food, and fragments of female nudes, his most imaginative pictures are those in which something outside easy comprehension seems to lurk. There is a sense of curiosity in his straight pictures with a latent expressionism. We can better understand his later accomplishments by recalling the ironic image-making of his early years, during which he glued together pieces of photographs to create an uneasiness. Enigma prevails in his close-ups of faces, including his own with cap and monocle. It adds interest to his pictures of light projected through a wicker basket, creating abstract patterns that seem unrelated to their source.

In 1933 Hausmann moved to Ibiza, where he stayed for three years. From this Mediterranean city he went to Czechoslovakia. After World War II he moved to Limoges, France, where he continued to photograph in an innovative fashion until his death in 1970.

HANS BELLMER, like Hausmann, went against the grain of conventional German society. The son of a Silesian engineer, he was directed by his father to study technology in Berlin. He rebelled by associating himself with Otto Dix and George Grosz, two of the most provocative artists in Berlin in the early 1920s. To Bellmer, like Grosz, sex was a symbol of decay.

An extremely talented draftsman, he became known for his drawings, paintings, and etchings of his »doll«. Fascinated with children's toys and Max Reinhardt's stage production of *The Tales of Hoffmann,* he fabricated a life-size doll out of papier-mâché and plaster that, by means of ball-joints, could assume many positions–both normal and bizarre. He shared Grosz's and Dix's distress at Hitler's rise to power, and in protest against Nazism he withdrew from society and devoted his time to photographing and drawing his artificial woman.

Bellmer photographed his creation in a variety of poses. These photographs–the first of which was reproduced in 1934 in the surrealist journal *Minotaure*–are more than mere recordings of the doll. They are jarring, mordant images that exude an eccentric sexuality often set against backgrounds that heighten their eroticism. In one instance he printed a negative photograph that parallels a surrealistic dream in which day turns into night.

The mannequin became a standard motif for surrealists and can be seen in photographs by Umbo, Coppola, and Citroen. Bellmer, however, more sensitively exploited the symbolism and ambiguity of lifelike figures than did any other photographer.

In 1937 Bellmer created a more complex jointed doll, which he also photographed extensively. He had long identified with the French surrealists and the following year he moved to Paris. In 1953 he returned to Berlin. In his later years he was confined to a psychiatric hospital.

HERBERT LIST is another German photographer who paid tribute to surrealism. He left Hamburg to attend the private school Johanneum in Heidelberg from 1921 through 1923. He was interested in literature, through which he became aware of the surrealists. He embarked on a successful career in the coffee business but left the field of commerce in the early 1930s to become a photographer.

List was neither interested in Berlin's cabaret scene nor in objective reportage nor new, dizzying perspectives. His photographs reflect international interest in surrealism, an interest underlying more photographic imagery than seems apparent at first. His surrealism represents a reality that encourages involvement, first with the eye and then the mind. We quickly identify the parts that make up his camera-made dreams, then marvel at the way he has brought them together. List's photographs hold our attention through strange juxtapositions and the telescoping of space. People in motion interact with objects in life and in dreams, creating a state of flux, but a photograph freezes everything into relationships that are forever static, making them somewhat formal. Often added to this is an arrangement of foreground elements used to cause the mind to deal with unexpected near/far relationships that recall the Daliesque deep-space school of surrealism. The clarity of List's pictures produces an intense physicality that is disquieting and mysterious. Yet unlike most innovative German photography between the wars, his is also rather lyrical. In 1936 List left Hamburg for London, then moved to Paris, where he primarily became a fashion photographer, making pictures that were well crafted, pleasant, and strong in design. Pictures of his post-German

VI. Hans Bellmer, The doll, ca. 1935

VII. Hein Gorny, Untitled, ca. 1932

period, made in Greece, incorporate daring compositions of unconventional subjects that evoke daydreams rather than nightmares. In the 1940s and 1950s List became well-known for his informal portraits of artists such as Picasso and Morandi. His interest in surreal situations continued. These photographs were of ordinary motifs given a special twist by incorporating unusual relationships of the commonest kind of subjects.

List traveled and photographed extensively in the Mediterranean and the Caribbean. He was active until five years before his death in 1975.

If an analogy with politics were applied to photography, HEIN GORNY, like Herbert List, would be considered a rightist, as opposed to leftists like Umbo and Kesting.

As a teenager in Hannover Hein Gorny became acquinted with modern art. By the mid-1920s he was photographing, and he soon fell under the influence of Renger-Patzsch. While not so adventuresome about new subjects as many of the avant-garde photographers, he nevertheless created a well-regarded and distinctive body of work in the 1930s. His pictures were often, but not exclusively, related to rural life, and consequently there is a pastoral quality to many of them. Forests, groves of trees, or individual trees,

often back-lighted, details of snow and ice, and animals were subjects he favored. His awareness of the new vision is apparent in his strongly patterned pictures to promote the sale of products. To capture a viewer's attention, he used repetition of shapes rather than extreme viewpoints or awkward movements recorded by high shutter speeds. After World War II he actively continued as a photographer.

MAX BURCHARTZ was, with Moholy and Finsler, one of the major teachers of photography who saw the medium's relevance to the new society and times in Germany. He taught at the Kunstgewerbeschule in Essen. He did some striking close-ups for exhibitions. The most famous of these photographs, almost a motif for the modern-photography movement, was his picture of half a young woman's closely cropped face, framed by a black hat. This picture was shown at the 1929 »Film und Foto« exhibition and was later blown up to over six feet high and placed above the entrance to the »Das Lichtbild« photography exhibition held in Essen in 1931.

Burchartz's straightforward photographs of machines were integrated with text in a new fashion through montage and collage. These pictures became a trademark for him. In keeping with the new typography and layout concepts a number of other photographers also used photographs with text, but Burchartz did his own photography for his clients instead of having a cameraman shoot pictures to suit his concepts of the catalog or poster. His individual photographs are bold, but his influence as a teacher and designer constitutes his major contribution to modern photography in Germany. Like Moholy, Burchartz thought that modern design had social value, for it symbolized the new acceptance of machines and products as contributing to a better life for people. The notion of humans controlling machines was powerfully symbolic in Burchartz's *Arbeitsplatz*. It was this concept that gave the Bauhaus and the other modern design schools in Germany their philosophical justification. It was felt that the precise forms shaped by machines and pristine, unadorned buildings would provide the proper environment in which society could flourish unoppressed. Elaborate ornamentation was equated with the decadence of the past, when most people served an elite class that surrounded itself with elaborate buildings and artifacts created to dazzle with their expensiveness. Because it was based on new technical advances and did not require skilled hands, photography was seen as an ideal means of creating pictures that were impersonal and not associated with the past. The clear-cut reality of the photograph had a social virtue in the eyes of Burchartz, Finsler, and Moholy–the teachers of many of the photographers who change the medium's direction in Germany.

ANTON STANKOWSKI was trained in photography and design by Max Burchartz at the Folkwangschule in Essen. Much of his best work was done in Zurich, beginning in 1929, when he was a painter and graphic designer, and lasting until 1937, when he moved to Stuttgart.

Due to Moholy's innovations, by the time Stankowski became a photographer, the question for all young photographers was how to photograph what was seen every day in a way that would depart from mundane reality but still incorporate recognizable qualities with which viewers could identify. Stankowski did not have a theme or message to convey, but he had a sophisticated sense of design and understood the workings of his cameras. He handled informal photographs of street incidents and very formal studio work for advertisements equally well. Each of his pictures has its own vitality. He achieved this effect by using slow shutter speeds, causing cars in motion to register on film as a blur while the lens recorded motionless elements clearly. Like many of the photographers in Germany, he photographed streets from high vantage points. In his case, however, shadows recall conflicts of forces rather than designs to flatten forms, as was the intent with many photographs of this nature.

Stankowski always had clients, for he was thoroughly professional and solved pictorial problems with imagination. He continued his work as a photographer into the 1950s. At present he lives in Stuttgart.

KLAUS WITTKUGEL, an eclectic modernist like Stankowski, also trained at the Folkwangschule. His work varies a great deal, for much of it was done for purposes other than self-expression. His semiabstract photographs were few, but in the most successful ones he detached forms from their normal associations so that he achieved an expression of nonspecific space, light, and forms. A traditional sense of perspective was deliberately broken down to allow these basic properties to assert themselves rather than serve as elements that described a scene or object. Such pictures were rarely attempted with the camera and were even more rarely successful. Of the utmost importance, however, is their existence as indicators of the younger generation's attempt in Germany to reconcile the seeming objectivity of the lens with the freedom of, say, Kandinsky's brush and that of other painters who were developing a truly abstract visual art analogous to music.

Women photographers such as Julia Margaret Cameron in England and Gertrude Käsebier in America were well regarded in the nineteenth century and early years of the twentieth century in Germany. In the 1920s and 1930s a considerable number of women photographers gained prominence, such as Lucia Moholy, Florence Henri, and Irene Bayer. Most of the women photographers had studios in Berlin, where there was a great demand for photography for advertising and onstage theater productions and personalities.

LOTTE JACOBI was an outstanding photographer. Her father, grandfather, and great grandfather were professional cameramen. The family studio was in Thorn, West Prussia. When she was two, her parents moved to Posen, where she studied art history and literature at the academy.

At eighteen she married a lumber merchant, leaving him soon after the birth of her son to move to Munich, where she spent two years studying commercial photography. In her first studio she employed the skills she had learned at the academy and those she had picked up as a child in her father's studio.

Jacobi's subjects came from the theatrical world of Brecht and Weill. Like Umbo, but with more warmth, she stylized her portraits by directing the lights to suggest a mask over the faces of her subjects. This sense of stage drama was accentuated by the cinematic device of moving in close or placing the face off center. She has said that the vogue in avant-garde photography in Germany for unusual placement of the head in a portrait played a relatively small part in her use of this device. She seems to have independently embodied in her work accents such as this to create what were thought of as »modern« portraits. It was not often her aim to lay bare her subject's soul in the fleeting moment during which she captured his or her likeness on glass plates. Rather than attempt to record a revealing moment, she viewed the face as a form to be placed in such a way as to catch the viewer's attention.

Her rather soft portrait of Käthe Kollwitz certainly engages our emotions, but most of her pictures are briskly succinct and summarize the »look« of her subjects with a minimum of character projection. She may fondly dwell on the features of a friend, as she did in the case of Lotte Lenya, but this was an exception, not the rule—possibly because she was dealing with film and stage impersonations rather than real people. She wanted to make strikingly theatrical photographs rather than capture personalities.

Jacobi came to New York in 1935 and established a studio with her sister, Ruth. She left the city in 1955 for Deering, New Hampshire, where she continues to be very active.

Another Berlin photographer whose reputation rested on her portraits of theater and film

VIII. Elli Marcus, Portrait Helene Weigel, 1930

personalities was ELLI MARCUS. Like Jacobi, she established her studio early in life. After a year as an apprentice in a portrait studio, she opened her own establishment at the age of eighteen and began specializing in stage photography. Her close-up pictures of actors were taken on stage with existing light during rehearsals, which was an unusual procedure. It allowed her to retain the drama associated with a role and also convey something of the personality of the performer outside of his or her stage persona. She used the technique of above-eye-level portraits, lights projected from below to cast unusual shadows, and a slightly overall softness to evoke the temporary taking on of the characteristics dictated by a playwright.

Like most Jewish photographers, Marcus left Germany when Hitler came to power. In 1933 she established a studio in Paris. When the German army overran France, she came to the United States. Fortunately, she was able to bring from Europe about one hundred fifty of her vintage portraits, which helped her establish herself in New York City.

Else Simon, who used the professional name YVA, was an imaginative Berlin photographer of the 1930s who specialized in nudes, portraits of dancers, and pictures of new fashions. Her achievements again emphasize the number of outstanding women photographers in Germany at this time. The most distinctive pictures she made were those in which she wove together the new contemporary design concepts–that is, image patterns and subtle theatrical lighting–to convey a sense of mystery and glamour. The work of Yva confirms that assignments for commercial work, such as pictures of accessories for a fashionable wardrobe, did not necessarily subordinate the creativity of a truly resourceful spirit. We know this was also the case with Edward Steichen in America and the German- and Russian-born photographers Horst Horst and George Hoyningen-Huene, who began their professional careers in Paris and then became very innovative fashion photographers in America. Yva found fashion photography not a bit constricting. She used an oblique approach to photography, in which she hinted at the glamour a women accrued while wearing this or that attire or adornment. Her lens was as exacting as Renger-Patzsch's, but her vision, feminine and sensuous, conferred a quality that is missing from almost all other German photography of the 1930s.

MARTA HOEPFFNER's most interesting photograms were stark portraits and those she did in homage to Wassily Kandinsky and Manuel de Falla. The first of these photograms recalls Kandinsky's late geometric paintings, which look like drawings for a network of city streets seen from above. The work honoring de Falla has a more lyrical quality, which is appropriate to the famous Spanish musician's rhythmic style. These images were made in a darkroom without a camera. Opaque forms were placed on a piece of photosensitive paper, then a white light was turned on to cast »white shadows«; this was followed by normal development. The results are close to semiabstract paintings. This might be expected from a former student of the abstract painter Willi Baumeister, who taught Hoepffner at the Kunstschule in Frankfurt. Her imagery is very similar to Viktor Eggeling's inventive abstract films made in the early 1920s, which she probably

knew, for they were highly acclaimed by El Lissitsky, Raoul Hausmann, and Fernand Léger and written about by contemporary critics. She has been an influential photography teacher for many years and is always associated with the traditions of avant-garde art.

MARIANNE BRESLAUER was one of the fortunate people who had every opportunity to learn about art from her earliest years. She was born in Berlin to a sophisticated professional family. Her father was a professor of architecture, and her mother's father was a prominent museum director. From 1927 to 1929 she studied in Berlin at an arts and crafts school. She next went to Paris, where she was much influenced by Man Ray, Paul Citroen, and Werner Rohde. In 1930 she returned to Berlin to work for the house of Ullstein. Her early photographs were often portraits of friends such as Umbo and Citroen. In 1929 and 1932 she photographed extensively in Paris. Between these years she worked in Jerusalem, Berlin, and various Italian cities.

If it can be said that Breslauer had a style, it was based on her immediate responses to events and to people rather than concern for the formal qualities of a situation or subject.

Her dramatic portrait of Citroen affirms her consciousness of surrealism but represents only a single facet of her wide-ranging work. Her pictures have the charm of fortuitous snapshots. When her subjects were important individuals from the world of art and politics, she had a sure eye for private moments during which these people were unaffected by their stature. Her photographs of objects also seem to have an informality that gives them a sense of fantasy. Switzerland served as a sanctuary for Breslauer. She worked primarily in Zurich, where she now lives.

AENNE BIERMANN, through her husband, Herbert Biermann, came in contact with members of the art world, including Franz Roh. She was primarily interested in music but taught herself photography in the mid-1920s and became known for her striking close-up portraits as well as her unusual treatment of other subjects. Her photographs of clusters of eggs and apples reflect, in their repetition, an interest in shape and texture. Details of an ashtray full of cigarette butts, ashes, and matches bring us up close to a subject less attractive than eggs and apples. The Merz collages of Kurt Schwitters come to mind, for he too created pictures of debris. Biermann utilized the camera's ability to record small things with great fidelity, so that when enlarged to greater-than-material size they expressed the nature of all kinds of subjects, both pleasing and displeasing. Renger-Patzsch had a similar aim, but he reserved this technique to convey the subtleties of nature's designs rather than use the camera's capacity to magnify small bits of debris to such accessible size that a viewer is obliged to contrast rubbish with more exalted material. In 1930 a monograph on Biermann's photographs was published–a distinction enjoyed by only a few photographers of the period.

ANNELIESE KRETSCHMER, another distinctive woman photographer, came from Dortmund, where she now lives in retirement. Her career in art began at the Kunstgewerbeschule in Munich in 1920. After two years she studied photography in Essen with L.V. Kaenal for two additional years. She then studied with Franz Fiedler in Dresden from 1924 to 1928, at which time she married the sculptor Sigmund Kretschmer. In 1934 she returned to her native Dortmund and established a photography studio in which she was active until 1975.

Kretschmer's work is unreservedly modern. Her mastery of design is especially impressive due to the size of some of her surviving vintage prints. Three to four times larger than most normal prints, they stand out because of the boldness of details and shadows she used to set off her commonplace objects. Details blend with blank or near-blank passages to convey a sense of surprise. We turn away from her pictures with a diagram of her black/white relationships still in our mind. They continue to engage our interest for a considerable length of time, due to her consistent power to make scale exaggerations more than just blow-ups. She was able to subvert the rigidity of the lens's indiscriminating view of all that was before it and charge her pictures with an aesthetic value quite apart from her nominal subjects.

In our discussion of avant-garde women photographers, we must be sure to include those who were influenced by the Bauhaus.

FLORENCE HENRI provided a link between photography at the Bauhaus and the innovative use of the camera in Paris. Born in New York, she was taken as a child to Europe by her French father and German mother. Henri, like a number of prominent American photographers such as Ansel Adams, Wynn Bullock, and Paul Caponigro, began her artistic career as a musician. She shifted to the visual arts in 1914, when she was 21. By 1918 she was associated with such dadaists as Hans Richter, Hans Arp, and John Heartfield. In 1921 she met Moholy in Berlin and a year later became a friend of Theo Van Doesburg. In 1924 she went to Paris to study painting with Fernand Léger and Amédé Ozenfant. As a result she developed a strong Purist style of semiabstract painting.

In 1927 Henri attended the Bauhaus in Dessau. At this time she began to use the camera seriously. The photographs she created at the Bauhaus and shortly thereafter in Paris were an innovative mix of constructivism and surrealism.

Her first photographs, in which she included mirrors, were made in 1927, while she was at the Bauhaus. These were published in *i10* in Amsterdam in 1928, with an introduction by Moholy. After she arrived in Paris, her imagery became more complex because she began to make collages of her photographs. The shadows she used as strong linear elements neutralize our orientation and cause us to wonder where her camera was in relation to her subjects.

Like so many of the avant-garde photographers of her day, Henri also did close-ups of faces. These evoke a matter-of-fact materiality that suggests she was more interested in the forms of the faces than in the individuality of her subjects. Quite three dimensional as compared to most close-ups, her photographs of fruit–out of which she created some of her collages–and people make use of the camera's ability to record textures and thus convey a sense of the surface.

After about 1938 Henri did less photography. She has recently been in poor health and is unable to paint or pursue other artistic activities in her home and studio south of Paris, where she has lived for many years.

GRETE STERN, who came from Wuppertal-Elberfeld, was attracted–as were many people–to the bright lights of Berlin. She attended the Kunstgewerbeschule in Stuttgart from 1925 to 1927, then studied photography privately in Berlin with Walter Peterhans. During the years 1929-1930 she was a student at the Bauhaus. In 1931 she opened a studio in Berlin with ELLEN AUERBACH and soon became known for her strikingly insightful portraits. She also did still-life and imaginative advertising photographs that often have an element of surrealism.

To create portraits that were unusual and avant-garde was difficult. A number of photographers, in fact almost all of them represented in this book, produced portraits. Renger-Patzsch's were strong, not because he intended them to be so, but because of his personality and aims as an objective reporter. Jacobi's and Marcus's were influenced by many of their subjects' being stage personalities.

Stern's portraits were just as objective as Renger-Patzsch's, but she used the sharp lens of her camera to reveal the subtle personal characteristics of the face for other purposes; her clear-cut portrait of Brecht marvelously confirms a fascination for this man. It smells of brown bread and onions. In it we see an intellectual with short hair, a middle-class collar, and eyes and a forehead that cannot but command our attention–so intensely set are the muscles in his face.

As more and more of the new-vision advertising photography comes to light, it will become apparent that a great deal of imagination was involved in creating photographs that would immediately attract a viewer's attention and then communicate a product's merits. Grete Stern and Ellen Auerbach were partners in one of the most innovative firms providing photographs of this nature. Because they had been nicknamed Ringl and Pit as children, they used these names for their studio. Studio Ringl & Pit worked with a great variety of clients, from cigarette manufacturers to distributors of petroleum products. Their solutions to the problem of product identity and means of catching a customer's eye were original and in keeping with the spirit of the new vision.

Grete Stern and her husband, HORACIO COPPOLA, an Argentinian, met in Berlin in 1931, after Coppola had studied photography with Stern's teacher, Peterhans. In the 1930s he used the skills he had learned in Peterhans's studio composition classes to produce imaginative, surreal-tinged photographs such as one of a doll with a crumpled dress stuffed in a box and others of household items–including an arrangement of an egg and a piece of string.

Coppola went with Stern to London in 1933, and in the mid-1930s they moved to Buenos Aires, where they were married. Since then he has been active as a photographer whose work has often been reproduced in books about Argentina.

GERTRUDE ARNDT was trained as a weaver. Her husband, ALFRED ARNDT, a painter and architect, was a master at the Bauhaus school. This may have influenced Arndt to explore through the camera the dynamic quality of life at the institution that gave special emphasis to integrating the various media. Her photographs reflect the 1928-1930 preoccupation with transforming ordinary subjects into strong visual

IX. Marianne Brandt, Stillife with Clock, ca. 1928

statements or catching on film a spontaneous gesture from an unusual viewpoint. She illustrates the impact that Moholy's ideas had on those who were open to new avenues of expression.

MARIANNE BRANDT was another craft student at the Bauhaus who became involved with photography. Many of her photographs were of metal objects seen up close. This interest in the surface of metals may stem from her work at the Bauhaus, where she was recognized as a very skilled worker in fine, unadorned metals. One of her pieces that has often been reproduced is of brass, sectioned off in geometric forms to create a half-globe teapot with ebony handles. The emphasis on the integration of form and the effects that could be gained by using polished metals carried over into her photography.

While referring to photographers who were at the Bauhaus, it should not be overlooked that teachers there who were not involved professionally with photography nevertheless did some very interesting work with the camera. JOSEPH ALBERS, while internationally famous as a painter for his investigations of color, was among those who did unusual work in photography while at the Bauhaus. Just as he extended his range of expression by designing glass vessels bound with German silver, he took artistic photographs. Among others whose major area of concern was not photography but who explored

the expressive possibilities of the camera were HAJO ROSE, GEORG MUCHE, ALBERT HENNIG, HERBERT SCHURMANN, and the husband and wife EDMUND COLLEIN and LOTTE GERSON. Another was EUGEN BATZ, whose photographs were quite surreal—which may mean that Peterhans played a role in his development. Moholy and constructivism were behind most of the imagery of those listed.

Moholy felt that the sensitivity of film and photo paper to light especially related photography to the post-World War I period. ALBERT RENGER-PATZSCH's view was that very detailed realistic photographs of small organisms in nature as well as photographs of products of technology would reveal that humankind's designs and nature's designs were often analogous.

Renger-Patzsch's book, *Die Welt ist schön (The World Is Beautiful)*, was published in 1928 and became one of the most influential books of the period. Through the words of the Lübeck art historian, Carl Georg Heise, and the pictures of Renger-Patzsch, the view was set forth that everything in the world was beautiful if one would just open one's eyes to the marvelous designs of people and nature.

Born to a cultured family in Würzburg, Renger-Patzsch learned the rudiments of camera operation while quite young. His early interest in both technology and nature never diminished. At the Kreuzschule in Dresden he emphasized classical studies, which perhaps accounted for his great love of order and clarity. After service in the German army, he returned to Dresden to study chemistry at Dresden Technische Hochschule (Dresden Technical College). In 1922 he became the director of the Folkwang Archives in Hagen. He left this post in 1925 to become an independent commercial photographer. During the same year his first book of photographs, *Das Chorgestühl von Cappenberg (The Choir Stalls of Cappenberg)*, was published. Renger-Patzsch caught the spirit of medieval art by selecting details of the beautifully carved wood sculptures that were part of the choir stalls. He found the subject a challenge to his concepts and carried the project off with a high level of technical proficiency. His next two books, published in 1927 and 1928, were *Die Halligen (The Islands of Schleswig-Holstein)*, and his classic, *Die Welt ist schön*, which clearly defined his style and spoke of photography as useful primarily for documentation.

To encourage this view of photography, Renger-Patzsch made the most straightforward of photographs so that the objects in front of his camera could express their beauty in almost clinical terms. Influenced by the tendency in the 1920s to rely on repetition of forms as a pictorial device, he photographed rows of related forms in as cool and dispassionate a manner as possible, to concentrate attention on the design of his subjects.

For the May 1929 issue of *Das Kunstblatt*, Gustaf Stotz, director of the »Film und Foto« exhibition, wrote of the new imagery that was being created by technical advances in camera equipment and better film at that time:

> A new optic has developed. We see things differently now, without painterly intent in the impressionistic sense. Today things are important that earlier were hardly noticed: for example shoe laces, gutters, spools of thread, fabrics, machines, etc. They interest us for their material substance, for the simple quality of the thing-in-itself; they interest us as means of creating space-form on surfaces. . . .[12]

Hardly a better description could be written of Renger-Patzsch's selection of subjects and dedication to an objective approach to photography. This objectivity is related to the Germanic love of accuracy and categorization. The camera, Renger-Patzsch felt, was the ideal instrument with which to acquaint the public with the pure object and extend human vision so that forms too small to see with the unaided eye could be examined and appreciated. He expressed in an essay he wrote in 1937 about the photographs in *Die Welt ist schön* the beliefs of what could be called a logician, so precise and logically related were his words to his pictures and so consistent with the rational side of German thought. For him, order and progress were two sides of the same coin. His use of almost slide-rule calculations when composing his photographs of ordinary things expands on awareness of textures and relationships of elements in buildings, machines, plants, and even animals.

Renger-Patzsch's pictures were viewed by the Germans as part of a larger order—much beyond the subjects photographed. The precise interrelatedness of parts became a symbol of the order many people felt would come to German society through advanced technology. It was the view of commentators and critics that exposure to photographs like those of Renger-Patzsch would increase the cohesiveness of society and encourage people to work concertedly for the common good. By inference, these photographs aimed to evoke pride in the success of German ingenuity in the manufacturing and marketing of new products and discourage any feelings of necessity to be individualistic and therefore disruptive.

Like the steady din of a smooth-running machine, these photographs tended to soothe and carry the message that all was well in Germany and would remain so if the rhythm were not disturbed. The country's leaders considered this to be a primary condition for the restoration of Germany's national pride and prosperity.

Renger-Patzsch worked in a style that is similar to an objective, technical drawing by an architect or designer made to give viewers the tangibility of an object's basic structure. The way he photographed his immobile and silent subjects provided a showcase for his special eye for design and for his sensitivity to the juxtaposition of textures. It is a paradox that Renger-Patzsch, who did not consider himself to be an artist, created work of aesthetic distinction. He consistently called attention to relationships of order and beauty that had been overlooked. He did this not by selecting new subjects but by the way in which he recorded buildings, machines, flowers, and mineral specimens.

Renger-Patzsch very sparingly used the classic dark/light of chiaroscuro to enliven his pictures. It was his usual practice to give equal emphasis to all elements. We find a kind of socialistic leveling of values without high or low lights in his homages to the engineers who designed the buildings and machines he so often took as his subjects. Although this emphasis on equality and unity of form prevented Renger-Patzsch from inventing new and dynamic relationships in his pictures, it allowed him to unite art and technology philosophically—an aim of many artists and architects in the 1920s.

In 1928 Renger-Patzsch moved to Essen, where he continued his own work in the studio and darkrooms of the Museum Folkwang. He remained active as a portraitist and commercial photographer and was in great demand by architects and manufacturers specializing in such items as glass vessels and machines. In the early 1930s he taught for a short time at the Folkwang-schule. He continued to photograph and publish attractive books on aspects of German architecture and related subjects, but it can now be seen that his contribution to the history of photography can be placed in the late 1920s and early 1930s.

In this period of vigorous German mercantilism, the visionary ERNST FUHRMANN saw in photographs not evidence of material successes but records that confirmed the grand process of creation. When young, he was unwilling to subject himself to the disciplines of regular schooling and was permitted by his parents to teach himself through extensive reading and travel to many parts of Europe. This born dreamer became haunted by the idea that the seemingly impenetrable maze of new knowledge about nature's root patterns could be put in order by a camera's recording details of the construction of plants and minerals. He disagreed with conven-

tional scientific explanations of the world's evolution, and the camera became a tool to confirm his ideas. He employed a number of photographers to carry out documentation. Among them was Renger-Patzsch. Taking close-ups of plants was fairly widespread in the 1920s and early 1930s. In America, Edward Weston and Imogen Cunningham made a great many of these photographs, but they were more like music than mathematics. This aim was more romantic than Fuhrmann's. The Americans were trying to find the simplest forms with which to express their love of nature rather than having an objective, scientific attitude toward what could be revealed by the camera.

Fuhrmann did not take any pictures himself, but he was very active in selecting the details to be photographed. His insistence upon the clarity of parts and the separation of tones was due to the fact that the photographs he commissioned were to be reproduced in books that explained his ideas. One of Fuhrmann's aims was to relate art objects to natural objects and compare botany with zoology, for he felt that plants could be structurally compared to animals. The pictures made for him incorporated details as well as the bold stylizations used in modern photographs. In addition, they are expressive of the interchange that occurred in Germany between the brilliant achievements of science and trends toward the use of efficient formats for housing and consumer products.

We now see that the pictures commissioned by this obsessive man penetrated beyond the rigid surfaces of his subjects—in the case of those made for him by Renger-Patzsch, this may be due to the photographer's sympathy toward Fuhrmann's views or the disciplined technique he applied to all kinds of subjects. Fuhrmann left Germany in 1938 and moved to New York, where he died in 1956.

KARL BLOSSFELDT's enlargements were also made to extend, through photography, what could be seen with the unaided eye—an aim of Renger-Patzsch and Fuhrmann. Blossfeldt's photographs, however, transcended his limited intentions.

He could be called the father of Neue Sachlichkeit photography, but this would not be true to his purpose. He was more interested in encouraging the development of a new Greek classicism than in developing objectivity. Before 1926 his pictures existed primarily as lantern slides made to be seen only by art and design students. He began his unique camera exploration of forms in nature before World War I, but the results were not widely known until 1928, when his most revealing book, *Urformen der Kunst (Original Forms of Art),* was published.

His early apprenticeship at an ironworks-where he first developed a responsiveness to curving, attenuated forms in nature–had a lifelong influence. His early art training was taken in Mägdesprung, during the period 1881 to 1884, after which he went to the Königliche Kunstgewerbeschule in Berlin to study sculpture and painting. After a trip to Italy, Greece, and Northern Africa, he began to photograph details of plants.

In 1898 be became a teacher at the school he had attended in Berlin. There he further developed his photographic techniques and taught the modeling of plant forms. The large selection of his plant photographs published in *Urformen der Kunst* struck a responsive chord in art and photography circles in the 1920s, when semiabstract form became an important means of expression.

Blossfeldt's taste for sinuous curves was undoubtedly initially fostered by the popular Jugendstil movement, which was at its peak of influence when he was a student in Berlin. By isolating greatly enlarged details of stems against a plain light background, he called attention to the process whereby buds and new leaves unfold as arching forms while maturing.

Blossfeldt's photographs raise a question wider than the history of photography: Did Jugendstil design, which grew out of a firsthand study of plant forms and photographs, influence abstract ornamental art and help to create a receptive climate for abstract art? A study of his photographs provides at least a partial answer, if one considers the nature of the forms found in the work of many painters in the 1930s and 1940s.

In Blossfeldt's prints, the lacelike filigree of nature's designs and the sheer »engineering« marvels found in plants were enlarged several times to provide intimate knowledge of what the camera recorded. The careful placement of similar forms facing each other, almost like personalities, suggests an identification of lower plant forms with human life. They were, however, primarily made to give ideas to craftsmen who were designing ironwork or wallpaper.

His second important book, *Wundergarten der Natur,* was published in 1932, the year of his death. In this book he stated his intent. »She (nature) is an educator about beauty and intrinsic feeling and a source of most noble delights. My documents of plants shall promote again the unity with nature. They shall rouse again the sense for nature, shall point at the over-rich treasure of forms in nature and stimulate our observations in our domestic world of plants.«[13]

In his portraits AUGUST SANDER exemplified, as no other photographer did, the special nature of German realism of the 1920s. Thus he is truly related to the Neue Sachlichkeit movement. The son of a miner, he never strayed far from the hard look on life that characterized the men who intimately knew the bowels of the earth. Like many professional photographers he began using the camera as an amateur. After military service and marriage he served an apprenticeship with a number of commercial photographers. His professional work began in Linz, Austria, but in 1910 he was able to establish his own studio in Cologne. To increase business, he traveled to surrounding towns and villages and created portraits. In 1918 he became acquainted with the painter Franz Wilhelm Seiwert, who felt that art should reflect society's structure. Inspired by his discussions with Seiwert, Sander began his great photographic project, *Menschen des 20. Jahr-*

X. August Sander, The Lord of the Manor and his Wife, ca. 1928

hunderts (Man of the 20th Century). This anthropological approach changed his method of working. No longer would he retouch his negatives to »improve« the appearance of his sitters. He began asking people from all strata of society to pose for him. Their likenesses were printed on smooth paper to reveal even warts. By 1929 he had completed enough of this project to publish Antlitz der Zeit (The Face of Time), a collection of objective photographs of people from all walks of life.

The stark force of Sander's polemical portraits is what places his work in the Neue Sachlichkeit movement. Unlike other portraitists of this period, such as Hugo Erfurth and Erna Lendai-Dircksen, he made no attempt to sentimentalize the myth of German society's strengths and weaknesses. As a result his pictures, more than any others, give us a fuller context of the collision between the comforts of the early land-oriented autocratic German culture and the promises of a bright future offered by the industrial twentieth century.

We may be guilty of reading too much underlying cynicism into his portraits, but we must remember that Sander was politically a liberal. During the 1920s, when these photographs were being made, Hitler was receiving more votes at each election, and political assassinations and acts of violence were taking place in large numbers. It should also be recalled that there were daily reports of other events that indicated serious instabilities in the society. All of this must be seen as a backdrop for Sander's portraits.

Judging from his approach to portraiture, Sander had humanistic insights that he did not allow to intrude into his work. He never sweetened the unpalatable nor romanticized his subjects in his quest for the basic patterns of class and status, which he saw symbolized in the poses assumed and the clothes worn by his subjects. Consequently, a sense of barely contained force hovers over some of his unflinching images. Only a few are seen as rebelling against the puritanical and pious class that dominated German society after Bismarck. People dressed in threadbare clothes are very rare in his photographs; the majority are obviously prosperous and self-satisfied. Even so, the collection of portraits conveys danger lurking in the shadows. The most striking of his photographs are those taken outside the studio, where the suggestion of the environment plays a major role in helping us to understand who the people are behind their masks.

Sander's sober style was essentially a means for probing his own psychological view of nationalism. His portraiture stands witness to his reading of the social conditions imposed by the time and by German traditions. We can now see that he unconsciously attributed his own anxieties to his subjects, and as a consequence his pictures are more subjective than has generally been considered. The emotionally charged edge to his work, which at its most potent level has the quality of a coiled spring, may speak of his rarely admitted concerns about the rumbling volcano that Germany was at that time.

Sander's intensity is most engaging when he was able to catch his subject gazing into the camera's lens with a mixture of fear and admiration for his or her pose or physical attributes. The grimly set features and rigid bodies we see in many of Sander's portraits are not so much the result of his demand that his sitter be still for a three-second exposure but of a fear of what might be recorded. Sander, like Christian Schad in his painted portraits of the 1920s, pinpointed a state of mind in Germany that derived from a loss of faith in traditional values. Sander thought of himself as a dispassionate classifier, taking neither a positive nor negative view of his sitters. In fact the implications and complications of life at that time were reflected the moment he chose to take portraits and in the responses of his subjects to being photographed.

One of Sander's sons was a leftist. As a consequence Sander was placed under close observation by the police in 1934, after Hitler came to power, and copies of *Antlitz der Zeit* were destroyed by the Nazis along with the printing plates. Fortunately, many of Sander's glass-plate negatives survived. He continued to take portraits, but they were not as strong as the work of the 1920s. He also took a large number of landscapes, which were published in the 1930s in a series of small booklets called *Deutsches Land/Deutsches Volk.* They are not avant-garde, as are his best portraits. It is often overlooked that as a commercial photographer he was sometimes commissioned to photograph architecture. In a few cases his interior details are outstanding and very much in tune with the new vision of Mantz and Renger-Patzsch. It has yet to be determined whether August Sander or his son made these pictures.

In the 1950s Sander largely discontinued taking photographs, devoting his time to organizing his archives. Honors began to be bestowed upon him by his own countrypeople as well as others, and his work became widely published.

By 1910 an appreciation for sequences, or groups of photographs as design elements in newspapers, had developed in England and France. International events in politics, art, and technology leading up to and taking place during World War I increased the use of photographs in newspapers. This development was limited, however, for the cameras used by the photographers serving the mass-circulation journals were cumbersome. Artificial light could be pro-

vided only by setting off magnesium powder in an open pan, which resulted in a flash of light and a cloud of acrid smoke, and temporarily blinded the subjects.

Newspaper photographers were barely tolerated by their colleagues, the reporters, because of the inability of cameras to catch newsworthy moments and the unpleasant results of the use of flash powder. This all changed in the 1920s. In Germany the compact Ermanox camera was introduced. It was equipped with a very fast f2.0 lens. Even on the relatively insensitive 4.5 x 6 cm glass plates used in this camera, it was possible to take interior pictures in available artificial light at shutter speeds of one-half to one-fourth of a second by using uranium intensification.

The man who made the most telling and imaginative use of this new camera was Dr. ERICH SALOMON, the son of a wealthy Berlin family. During the post–World War I inflation period, his family fortunes diminished drastically, and he took a job in Berlin in the publicity department of Ullstein Verlag, the largest publishing house in the world. There he became aware of the sales potential of news photographs. On one occasion in Berlin he heard that a large tree had fallen into a municipal bath, killing a woman. He hired a photographer to record the scene and sold the resulting picture at a good price. Soon afterward, to eliminate the cost of hiring a photographer, he took up the camera himself, for he had learned that he could sell his pictures for much more than he was paid for work at the publishing house. He quickly became a major photographer.

Soon Salomon was given a chance to take photographs for the *Berliner Illustrirte Zeitung,* one of Ullstein's publications and the Berlin periodical that used the greatest number of photographs. With his upper-class manners, a gift for persuasive conversation in seven languages, and the insight gained from his university training, he had a great success at capturing with his camera politicians and members of high society talking together in unguarded moments. It was necessary to steady his small camera on a tripod behind a convenient curtain or beside a sofa, but so accustomed were the statesmen to press photographers with large cameras that they ignored the well-dressed Salomon as he took their picture. His candid pictures of famous as well as ordinary people became widely known for giving readers of the *Berliner Illustrirte Zeitung* a feeling of being present at international conferences, court actions, and other rarely photographed events.

Salomon's quick responses, academic knowledge about the people he was photographing, and willingness to wait for a revealing moment to click his shutter helped to create the new profession of photojournalism. He was, like Felix H. Man and Tim Gidal, one of many German photographers who took up the camera as a means of livelihood during the bleak days of the 1920s, when academically trained men were unable to find jobs in their chosen fields. Due to their fresh approach a new style of photography began to appear in extensively illustrated publications in Munich and Cologne as well as Berlin.

Hardly less important to the history of photojournalism than Salomon was Hans Felix Sigismund Baumann, known today as FELIX H. MAN. He came from Freiburg, Breisgau, a town on the edge of the Black Forest. During World War I he served as an officer in the German army. While stationed on the Western Front he began to take photographs with a Vest-Pocket Kodak. After the war he resumed art studies begun in Munich and Berlin. In 1926 he settled in Berlin as an illustrator and graphic designer. He first began to use photographs as quick »sketches« for his illustrations. Soon he gave up drawing and became a photographer. His work with Berlin periodicals brought him into contact with »Dephot« (Deutscher Photodienst), a prominent photography agency serving various periodicals. The founder of this firm, Simon Guttmann, introduced Man to Stefan Lorant, the Berlin editor of *Münchner*

Illustrierte Presse. Lorant was impressed by his eye and gave Man assignments to do picture stories. In the period 1929-1931 he did more than eighty projects for *Münchner Illustrierte Presse* and *Berliner Illustrirte Zeitung,* the illustrated weekly that also employed Erich Salomon.

Like Salomon, Man used the Ermanox but found the Contessa-Nettel his most valuable camera for catching a dramatic movement or viewpoint. Exploiting the small size, large lens, and relatively fast glass plates and films used in these cameras, he photographed people with the light available as they went about their daily business. Combined in picture stories, these informal photographs often appeared in sequence in two-page spreads or captioned layouts. The presence of the camera was never acknowledged in his pictures—a factor that gave them a special psychological hold on those who saw them. The viewers became, in their mind, almost participants or at least first-hand observers of what Man had photographed. The candidness of his photographs was impressive, as was his ability to convey to viewers a sense of being in the presence of eminent as well as ordinary people.

For him the best time to release his shutter was based on Lessing's »fruitful moment« as described in his *Laocoon.* This would later be called »the decisive moment« by Henri Cartier-Bresson. It was Man's hope to get beyond a subject's facade and, through pictorial means, evoke more than mere surface appearances. This required great patience and an eye for that certain moment when this kind of psychological penetration was possible. The technical difficulties were many, especially when using existing artificial light inside buildings. Man started with a Contessa-Nettel camera for his first indoor essays, equipped with an f2.8 lens that took 6 x 9 cm glass plates. The larger size of the glass-plate negative caused him to prefer this camera over the Ermanox, even though the smaller camera had a larger lens. All his indoor essays had to be made on a tripod, for the exposures were

XI. Berliner Illustrirte Zeitung, »Greta Garbo in Holiday«, 1932

XII. Münchner Illustrierte Presse, 1931

between one fourth and a full second. It was not until 1932 that he turned to the Leica, when faster film became available.

His pictures acquainted millions with the world's leaders caught off-guard, while less well-known people were seen going about their everyday business. After his very successful career in Germany, Man moved to London, where his talents were recognized and his pictures used in British newspapers and magazines. In recent years he has largely given up photojournalism and has become famous in a second career. He is a leading authority on the history of lithography, the graphic process that became popular in the early years of the nineteenth century, just as photography made its appearance.

The work of three other well-regarded German pioneer photojournalists should be mentioned.

They are Alfred Eisenstaedt, Wolfgang Weber, and Bernd Lohse. Eisenstaedt became a renowned photographer for *Life* magazine. As a consequence some of the new attitudes toward photojournalism spawned in Germany flourished in the United States under editors influenced by Man's imaginative editor, Stefan Lorant, who did much to make *Münchner Illustrierte Presse* an exciting publication.

TIM GIDAL was another of the fraternity of photographers who created photojournalism. He did his first photoreportage for the *Münchner Illustrierte Presse* in 1929. Due to the favorable reception of this early work, he was sent on assignments to many parts of Europe, India, and the United States. The human condition was his main subject. Gidal, like Man and Salomon, was an intellectual and with the camera brought to his reportage a worldwide concern for the implications of political strife and the social events of the early 1930s.

Like many of his contemporaries who took pictures of people, Gidal liked to test the flexibility of the medium. His photogram self-portrait and some very design-oriented images testify that there were other facets to his work. His academic training, which included art history, gave him an awareness of form as a basic ingredient in all art.

In 1936 Gidal emigrated to Palestine, where he lived for two years. During World War II he was a photoreporter with the British Eighth Army. After the war he worked for *Life* until 1954. Since 1969 he has been photographing for books on children of many lands.

MARTIN MUNKACSI was a special kind of photojournalist and had unusual talent. He began his career in Budapest as a sports cameraman, then he progressed to wider fields of photography. His success encouraged him to expand his horizon and seek assignments in Berlin in 1927. Editors at the Ullstein Verlag were impressed by his press clippings and gave him a three-year contract, sending him to work for their publications *Die Dame, Koralle, Uhu,* and *Berliner Illustrirte Zeitung.*

Although not nearly as well-known today, Munkacsi's innovative photographs, at their best, match the verve of Henri Cartier-Bresson's work of the 1930s. There is a very distinctive controlling order to Munkacsi's pictures. This is truly remarkable, given the varied movements of many of his subjects. The forces of energy involved are not only conveyed by the stop-action made possible by a 1/1000 of a second shutter speed but also by the psychological impact of the arrangements of various forms within his pictures. Beyond technical virtuosity, there is, in his photographs, a very active surface design that quivers with a sense of movement quite distinct from the actions being caught by his camera's shutter. His photographs were directly expressive of the freedom of movement made possible by new cameras, fast shutters, and more light-sensitive film. Munkacsi's pictures were a result of an instinct for fresh and radical viewpoints that would give zest to current events of the day when reproduced in popular magazines and newspapers. His way of creating dimension and animating shapes reminds one of the complex figure lithographs by Lautrec. To escape the Nazis, Munkacsi came to the United States in 1934, where Carmel Snow, the very perceptive editor of *Harper's Bazaar,* hired him as her star fashion photographer.

He was one of the first photographers to do fashion photography outside the studio and to incorporate bird's-eye and frog's-eye views of models wearing the newest styles. In the mid-1940s Dr. Agho, art editor of *Vogue,* said in a lecture that »Munkacsi's coming to America was the most important thing that has happened to American photography in the past ten years«.[14] His approach to fashion photography was very new and impressive to younger American photographers like Richard Avedon, who learned much about the flexibility of the camera as a tool for recording that which the design of a dress or coat revealed.

XIII. Umbo, The hat, ca. 1927

UMBO, the name Otto Umbehrs used as a photojournalist, was another innovator in photojournalism. A native of Düsseldorf, he first studied painting and design at the Bauhaus from 1921 to 1923, then in the mid-1920s became connected with the film industry in Berlin. In 1926 he worked with Paul Citroen as a portrait photographer. His period as a photojournalist began in 1928, when the field was new. There was no delicacy about Umbo's stark photographs of people–the subject he employed so distinctly. His was a kind of slangy photojournalism. He continuously explored the range of possibilities of the films and cameras of the time, not as a technician, but as a poet. He learned how to characterize in graphic terms the collective state of mind behind the glittering, brittle facade of German prosperity. The barest essentials were for him enough to convey human joys, passions, fears, and pains. His pared-down vocabulary and cut-off forms of faces recall film close-ups seen for a fraction of a moment but retained in the mind for hours. Frequently, his pictures were made under low light conditions or with dramatic contrasts between highlights and shadows. This gave his men and women the look of having been caught in a flicker of light in a cellar nightclub. It was as if Umbo had the eyes of a bat and was acutely responding to the vibrations and smallest movement of his prey. His photographs sum up the passions of the time's far offbeat music, daring theater productions, and the brash Berliners' philosophy of »anything goes.«

The gritty authenticity of Umbo's pictures predicted some of the strong imagery of later photojournalists that gave visual expression to Germany's collective frustrations. They are a montage of the reactions of people swept up in a complex and eventually deadly confrontation between freedom—as exemplified by the art world in Berlin—and a dictatorship of the most destructive nature.

His portraits—or more properly, heads of people—are very close in spirit to the pre-World War I woodcuts and lithographs of expressionist artists such as Ernst Ludwig Kirchner and Karl Schmidt-Rottluff.

Umbo continued to work after World War II and was actively sorting his files and supervising the printing of his negatives in Hannover when he died in 1980.

Umbo's friend PAUL CITROEN, a Berliner, left school at fourteen to be an artist. During World War I he made contact with the *Der Sturm* group and by 1918 was involved in the dada movement in Berlin. In 1922 he became a student at the Bauhaus and became acquainted with Moholy. His photographic work began in 1925.

Citroen's imagery was often surreal, ranging from pictures of people and unusual views of life in city streets to still lifes. His photographs of people are informal, often close up and fragmentary—as if they had been cut out of a film. His use of shadows across parts of the face and the feeling of restricted space convey a stark new reality that suggests that volatile era during which they were created. In his pictures the viewer senses buoyancy but also the uneasiness that prevailed during that time of German history. The rawness of his fascinating, direct pictures is intensified by the feeling that he probed for meaning in the dim world with which he became acquainted in Berlin. A sense of immediacy is imparted by the lack of sharpness of his portraits—

as if he did not have time to set up for a conventional picture, so intent was he in recording his gut responses to what he saw.

The most provocative of his still lifes is that of a mannequin dressed in a white undergarment that does not quite cover the breasts. Her face is realistic, but we are aware that she is a mannequin because of the exposed joint at her shoulder. Her curved form was photographed against a severe rectangular element that accentuates the difference between feminine characteristics and geometry, creating an enigmatic and very surreal image. Citroen gave up photography in 1935 but continues his other artistic interests. He lives in Wassenaar.

FRIEDRICH SEIDENSTÜCKER, while not truly a photojournalist, became well-known for his published photographs of people. His mastery of the »caught« moment gave his photographs a wonderful sense of freshness and life. Seidenstücker was born in Unna/Westfalen but studied and lived most of his life in Berlin. He followed in the footsteps of Heinrich Zille, the famous early twentieth-century chronicler of Berlin's people, who made photographs to preserve information he wanted to include in his candid genre drawings. Seidenstücker's use of light to model forms reveals his training as a sculptor. He began creating photographs to serve as sketches. Some of the pictures he took of animals were applauded and published. Since little of his sculpture sold, he became a photographer. His solid slices of everyday life are informative without being dramatic. He conveyed a sense of animation in the way his camera recorded garments responding to the stresses of human anatomy in motion or in strained positions. While he took many pictures of workers, his pictures were not a general comment upon society. This places him closer to Eugene Atget than to Lewis Hine in his attitude toward people going about their everyday business.

Seidenstücker learned the new photographic language early in its evolution. He used a high viewpoint, found unusual repetitions of shapes, and effectively employed the fast shutter speeds with which cameras were then being equipped. His sure grasp of these new, and sometimes primitive, ways to record life gave his pictures a sense of emotional excitement in keeping with the times. He did not attempt to deeply engage his viewers with his subjects. His are spontaneous rather than carefully structured images. The camera seemed to amplify a responsive spirit that in turn provided a lively feeling of participation for his viewers. His photographs–because they are photographs and hence very believable–are emphatically exciting even now and retain their freshness. For instance, young women jumping over puddles of water was made, by his acute eye, into something much more than an example of stop-action photography. In our mind we help them jump; we feel the spring in our knees as the young women stretch their legs to carry themselves across the small stream. As subject matter for the camera in the 1920s, these images prefigure Cartier-Bresson's famous photograph of 1932 in which a man is leaping into a puddle of water. The works of Cartier-Bresson and Seidenstücker engage our physical being as well as our emotions.

Seidenstücker made informative and well-structured sequential pictures of men at work. One of the most unusual is a series of photographs of house painters. In these he made effective use of the viewpoints seen by house painters as they looked up and down from their ladders. The patterns created by the ladders leaning against the houses and the shadows of the ladders in the street were used in a contemporary way. Seidenstücker's photographs were included in books and periodicals published in Berlin, Essen, Frankfurt, and Stuttgart during the 1920s period of exuberance and even in the 1930s when Hitler came to power. After the defeat of Germany in 1945 he spent five years photographing the devastation of his adopted city. He continued to be an active photographer until 1955. In his last years he began to receive the recognition for his valuable contribution to German photography over a period of four decades. He died in 1966.

This survey of avant-garde photography in Germany between 1919-1939 provides a different view than has generally been held. We see that a very wholehearted commitment to practical, straightforward realism on one hand and experimental use of the camera and photosensitive materials on the other resulted in images that were related to vital art movements and social changes as well as new scientific attitudes toward matter and time.

With energy and determination a small group of men and women in Germany transformed photography into a medium that in many ways reflected the new world that took shape after 1919. Moreover, it becomes apparent only through their pictures that American photography in the post-World War II period embodied many qualities found in the inventive German photography that developed in the 1920s. When explaining many of the characteristics of American landscape photography, historians have rightly stressed a debt to Timothy O'Sullivan and Carleton E. Watkins and centered on Alfred Stieglitz and Paul Strand when dealing with other aspects of the medium in the early years of this century. Today we see that their work does not explain much that has happened in this country's photography during the 1960s and up to the present time. The influence of László Moholy-Nagy and the innovative uses of photography for communication that first took place in Germany have been underplayed.

In 1928 Moholy gave up teaching at the Bauhaus, moved to Berlin, and became engaged in various design projects as well as filmmaking. With Hitler's rise to power in 1933, he moved to Amsterdam, where he concentrated on design work. In 1935 he settled in London, where he continued his design activities and did photographs for three books: *Street Markets of London, Eton Portrait,* and *Oxford University Chest.*

In 1937 Moholy was invited to Chicago, at Walter Gropius's suggestion, to direct a new design school that was sponsored by the Association of Arts and Industries. The New Bauhaus: American School of Design, as it was called, started off well but collapsed at the end of the first year due to financial difficulties. Throughout 1938 Moholy sought support for another school in Chicago. He met with success and in the fall of 1939 opened the School of Design. After an uncertain beginning the new enterprise was given assurance of financial support by Walter Paepcke, president of the Container Corporation of America. Paepcke felt that good design was justified by its own merits in commerce and industry. He was also much impressed by Moholy's integration of new design concepts, new materials, and new approaches to the teaching of design for industry and marketing. In 1944, with Paepcke's help, the School of Design was reorganized into the Institute of Design. Moholy headed the school until his death in 1946.

Moholy successfully transplanted the concepts of the new vision in photography to America. His teaching shaped a view of photography's potential as an expressive medium—a view that continues to be a source of inspiration and philosophical inquiry thirty-five years after his death.

Moholy's ideas about the role of photography were disseminated to a relatively small number of American students at the New Bauhaus. Important to the history of American photography is that two of the students, Arthur Siegel and Henry Holmes Smith, became teachers of postgraduate students. After Moholy's death, his ideas about the medium's possibilities and his basic philosophy continued to be fostered by Harry Callahan and Aaron Siskind at the Institute of Design and later at the Rhode Island School of Design, where they both taught after leaving Chicago.

Henry Holmes Smith taught at the New Bauhaus and was a student there as well. He had known Moholy's work through his publications and made contact with him when he arrived in Chicago from England. At the time, Smith was working in the darkroom of a portrait studio in Marshall Field's department store. When Smith told Moholy of his experience with photography and described his admiration for the new vision Moholy had helped to establish in Germany, he was asked to design and install a darkroom for the new school. In 1947 Smith joined the art department faculty at Indiana University and carried the spirit of the Bauhaus to that institution. There he became the teacher of such innovative photographers as Betty Hahn, Robert Fichter, and Jerry Uelsmann, who later became influential teachers themselves.

The impact of Bauhaus ideas on Siegel was equally important. For more than twenty-five years he taught at the Institute of Design, subscribing to many of Moholy's ideas and using classroom problems that had evolved out of the Bauhaus curriculum. In 1964 Harry Callahan was hired by Moholy to teach at the Institute. Callahan likewise incorporated Moholy's Bauhaus concepts in his teaching methods. He brought Aaron Siskind to teach at the Institute of Design in 1951. Siskind, intimately acquainted with the avantgarde artists in New York City, added another facet of the experience offered to students. In his teaching he also maintained the use of many of Moholy's early Bauhaus problems.

William Larson, who arrived at the Institute of Design to do postgraduate work in 1966, has recalled the educational environment there and the openness to new ideas. He recently wrote, »The Moholy influence was both formal in its lineage and spiritual in its impact. . . . All attitudes toward picture-making were not merely tolerated but encouraged and supported in the best sense of the word.«[15] While following diverse paths, many of the graduate students who studied with Siegel, Callahan, and Siskind continued the Bauhaus tradition when they became teachers in university art departments and art schools in all parts of the United States. The openness to innovation and wholehearted acceptance of mixed media and experimental directions in their own work and that of their students has characterized · the paths later followed by influential Institute of Design graduates such as Thomas Barrow, Keith Smith, Linda Connor, Ray Metzker, Barbara Crane, William Larson, Charles Swedlund, and John Wood, among others. Through these teachers the imprint of Moholy and the new vision that originated in Germany has become deeply imbedded in American photography.

F O O T N O T E S

1   This survey of German photography exhibitions in the 1919-1939 period is based on Ute Eskildsen's essay »Innovative Photography in Germany between the Wars«, published in the catalog for *Avant-Garde Photography in Germany 1919-1939*, an exhibition organized by the San Francisco Museum of Modern Art in 1981.

2   Quoted in: *Photographische Industrie,* Number 35 (August 28, 1929).

3   Ibid.

4   *Die Form,* 1926, Number 12, p. 275-276.

5   Catalog *Avant-Garde Photography in Germany 1919-1939* (San Francisco Museum of Modern Art, 1981), p. 40.

6   L. Moholy-Nagy, *Malerei, Fotografie, Film* (München: Albert Langen Verlag, 1925), p. 32.

7   Ibid, p. 59.

8   A. Renger-Patzsch, »Ziele«, *Das deutsche Lichtbild,* 1927, p. 18.

9   *Die Wochenschau,* 1931, Number 29, p. 5.

10   Jan van der Marck, Herbert Bayer: *From Type to Landscape* (Hanover, N.H.: Hopkins Center, 1977), p. 22.

11   Marc Scheps, *Tim Gidal* (Jerusalem: The Israel Museum, 1975), p. 41.

12   Gustav Stotz in: Kunstblatt, May 1929.

13   Karl Blossfeldt, *Wundergarten der Natur,* Berlin 1932.

14   Recalled in conversation with the author, April 1980.

15   Letter from William Larson, Wyncote, Pennsylvania, September 1980.

B I O G R A P H I C A L
I N F O R M A T I O N

HERBERT BAYER Born 1900, Haag, Austria. In 1919 after service in the Austrian army, he became an apprentice to an architect in Linz. The following year he assisted the architect Emanuel Margold in graphic design in Darmstadt. During the years 1921-1923 he attended the Bauhaus. In 1925 he was appointed a master at the Bauhaus, to teach typography and advertising layout. In 1928 he moved to Berlin, where he worked as a graphic designer and exhibition architect. It was during the period 1928-1938 that he became involved with photography. He moved to New York in 1938 and designed the exhibition »Bauhaus 1919-1928« for the Museum of Modern Art. From 1946 to 1976 he was design consultant and architect for the Aspen Institute for Humanistic Studies. He is now retired and lives in Montecito, California.

IRENE BAYER Born 1898, Chicago, Illinois. She grew up in Hungary but went to Germany in 1920 to study commercial art. After a year and a half in Berlin she visited Weimar, to see an exhibition of the objects being created at the Bauhaus. Much impressed, she went to Paris, where she met Léger and Picasso and attended lectures at the Sorbonne and Ecole des Beaux-Arts. In 1924 she returned to Weimar and in 1925 married Herbert Bayer. To assist him, she learned photographic techniques at the Leipzig Academy. With Bayer she returned to the United States in 1938. She divorced Bayer in 1944. After World War II she returned to Germany as a translator and became Chief of the American Photo Section in Munich. In 1947 she returned to the United States. She is now retired and lives in Santa Monica, California.

HANS BELLMER Born 1902, Katowice, Silesia, Germany. In 1923 he began to study engineering in Berlin, where he met the painters George Grosz and Otto Dix. He soon gave up engineering to become a typographer and illustrator. In 1933 he constructed a large doll to serve as a motif for his work. In 1934 he published a book about this doll, illustrated with his photographs. A second more flexible doll with a central ball-joint was constructed in 1937, which he photographed extensively. He left Berlin for Paris in 1938 and became more closely associated with the

surrealists. In 1949 *Games of the Doll* was published. It combined Eluard's poetry and Bellmer's hand-colored photographs of his second doll. He died in 1975 in Paris.

KARL BLOSSFELDT Born 1865, Schielo, Germany. From 1882 to 1885 he was apprenticed as a craftsman at the ironworks in Mägdesprung. Beginning in 1886 he studied sculpture and painting for four years at the Royal Museum of Arts and Crafts in Berlin. In the early 1890s he began taking photographs of plants to aid in the teaching of modeling at the school in Berlin where he was trained. When this school became the Hochschule für bildende Künste, he was appointed a full professor. He continued to systematically photograph details of plants in order to make lantern slides to show his students, to acquaint them with the structures of forms that could be used as a basis for decorative designs. He died in Berlin in 1932.

MARIANNE BRESLAUER Born 1909, Berlin, Germany. In 1927 she became acquainted with Umbo and Paul Citroen as well as with many other members of Berlin's avant-garde. Paris attracted her next. There she came in contact with Man Ray and Werner Rohde in 1929. She photographed Paris extensively and made informal portraits of prominent artists and dealers and their families. During 1930 and 1931 she was back in Berlin but also traveled to Italy and Jerusalem. The following year she returned to Paris and continued to take informal portraits of well-known people such as Picasso and Ambroise Vollard. In 1936 she left Germany for Amsterdam. From the Netherlands she moved to Zurich, where she now lives.

MAX BURCHARTZ Born 1887, Elberfeld, Germany. He began his career in art in his home city, where he attended the Kunstgewerbeschule. From 1906 to 1909 he was a student at the Kunstakademie in Düsseldorf. After leaving Düsseldorf he lived in Munich, Paris, and Berlin while developing his talents as a painter. During World War I he served in the army. Soon after the war he moved to Hannover, where he became acquainted with Kurt Schwitters. From Hannover he moved to Weimar in 1921 and became a follower of Theo Van Doesburg. With Johannes

Canis he founded an advertising agency in 1924. In 1926 he was appointed a professor at the Folkwangschule, to teach graphic design, typography, and photography. In 1933 he was forced out of this position at the Folkwangschule and until 1939 he had a private design studio. During World War II he again served in the army. In 1959 he was reappointed to teach an introductory course as well as graphic design and photography at the Folkwangschule. He died in 1961 in Essen.

PAUL CITROEN   Born 1896, Berlin, Germany. In 1910 he left school to become an artist. By 1914 he had met the painter Georg Muche and soon became acquainted with the group that was involved with »Der Sturm.« During the last year of World War I he made contact with the dada group in Berlin. In 1922 he enrolled at the Bauhaus. His work in photography extended over the period 1925 to 1935. He continued his other artistic interests until recent years. He now lives in Wassenaar.

HORACIO COPPOLA   Born 1906, Buenos Aires, Argentina. Coppola started work in photography in 1928. While traveling through Europe in 1931, he joined Bauhaus as a student of Walter Peterhans. Through him he met Grete Stern, his future wife. They moved to London in 1933 and later settled in Buenos Aires. There they founded a studio for advertising and photography in 1937. He has illustrated several books and is the author of numerous articles and monographs. He is still actively involved with photography in his home of Buenos Aires, Argentina.

ALFRED EHRHARDT   Born 1901, Triptis/Thüringen, Germany. After studying music and art and following a training in painting and graphics in Hamburg, he attended the Bauhaus in Dessau from 1927 through 1928. He was a pupil of Schlemmer, Albers, and Kandinsky. He then worked as a freelance artist in Hamburg until 1931 when he took on a professorship of materialism at the Hamburg Landeskunstschule through 1933. From then until 1935 he was a professor at the Danish academy in Asco. He then returned to Germany and began his extended study of nature and landscape photography. In 1937 his first book of plates appeared entitled *Das Watt. Kurische Nehrung* followed in 1938, and in 1939 *Island*. Along with landscape photography, he became increasingly absorbed in macro- and microscopic pictures (his publications include: *Kristalle,* 1939, and *Muscheln und Schnecken,* 1941). His first documentary film on this subject appeared in 1937. From 1945 this constituted his main area of work. Subsequently he has been awarded many film prizes both at home and abroad. He now lives in Cuxhaven.

ANDREAS FEININGER   Born 1906, Paris, France. He attended the Bauhaus in Weimar and a technical school in Zerlist, Germany, and graduated in architecture. Because his father, the prominent painter Lyonel Feininger, was American born, Andreas was an American citizen. Because there were not many jobs for architects in Germany, he went to the United States in 1928 but with little success. Self-trained as a photographer but knowledgeable about Moholy's work, he began using the camera. At first this was for reference purposes.

Upon his return to Europe in 1931, he worked with Le Corbusier's architecture office in Paris on a voluntary basis. Sweden was his next stop. In Stockholm, drawing on the skills learned at the Bauhaus, he took a job as a pottery designer, but this was not satisfactory. He next turned to commercial photography in Sweden. This led to his being a photographer who used superrealism and the manipulation of negatives as a means of giving distinction to his work. He returned to the United States and became a *Life* magazine photographer and began writing books, the first of which was *New Paths in Photography* (1939). There are now over a dozen books carrying his name, and his photographs have been frequently included in major American and European photography exhibitions at such museums as the Museum of Modern Art, International Museum of Photography, and Smithsonian Institution. He is now semiretired and lives in New York.

T. LUX FEININGER   Born 1910, Berlin, Germany. In the years 1928-1929 he was a student at the Bauhaus, where be became involved with photography. He photographed for Oskar Schlemmer special effects developed in the school's theater workshop and took innovative photographs of the Bauhaus jazz band. In the early 1930s his photographs were distributed to publications throughout Germany. Gradually, in the 1930s he turned from photography to painting. Because his father was American born, Lux came to the United States. He is now retired and lives in Cambridge, Massachusetts.

WERNER DAVID FEIST   Born 1909, Augsburg, Germany. During 1928 and 1929 he was a student at the Bauhaus. Peterhans was his teacher in photography. From the Bauhaus he went to Prague, where he worked as a graphic designer and advertising photographer. When the German army occupied Czechoslovakia in 1939, he quickly left the country, losing all his photographic equipment in the process, and joined the British army. After World War II he was an art director in London and in 1951 moved to Canada, where he served as an art director and graphic designer. He now lives in Montreal.

HANS FINSLER Born 1891, Zurich, Switzerland. Initially, he studied architecture but turned to art history under the direction of Heinrich Wölfflin during World War I. In 1922 he became a teacher and librarian at the Burg Giebichenstein Kunstgewerbeschule, near Halle, Germany, where he also taught photography. He returned to Zurich in 1932, where he founded a department of photography at the Kunstgewerbeschule. He died in 1972 in Zurich.

TIM GIDAL Born 1909, Munich, Germany. His academic studies in Munich were in the fields of history, economics, and art history. In 1929 he began to use the camera as a means of making money. He became a well-regarded photojournalist and frequently contributed to such periodicals as the *Berliner Illustrirte Zeitung* and *Münchner Illustrierte Presse.* By 1933 he was living in London, forced out of Germany by the Nazis. From 1936 to 1938 he lived in Jerusalem, then he returned to London where he did work for *Picture Post* and other pictorial journals. During World War II he was chief reporter in the Near East for the British Army's illustrated magazine, *Parade.* At present he is still active as a photographer and is a senior lecturer for visual communications at the University of Jerusalem.

HEIN GORNY Born 1904, Witten an der Ruhr, Germany. In 1922 he went to Hannover, where he first developed an interest in modern art. He learned as much from travel as from schooling. In 1924 he went to Italy and Egypt and went to Greece the following year. He was influenced by Albert Renger-Patzsch's ideas about photography in 1927, when he met him personally. By 1929 he was an established photographer in Hannover, and his work began to be seen in a wide variety of publications including the international annual *Photographie.* In 1930 he took a trip to Russia and in 1934 worked in Switzerland. On all of these trips he was very active as a photographer. In 1934 he tried to get established in Paris but failed and went to St. Moritz to do publicity photography. He took over Lotte Jacobi's studio in Berlin in 1935, when she left for America. He made a brief trip to the United States in 1939, but even with war on the horizon he returned to Germany, because his wife, Ruth Lessing, daughter of Theodor Lessing, could not secure a visa to travel. After World War II he served as an advertising photographer for such firms as A.J. Byers. He continued his activities as a photographer until his death in 1967.

JOHN GUTMANN Born 1905, Breslau, Germany. From 1923 to 1927 he studied at the State Academy of Arts and Crafts, Breslau. He was a master student under Otto Müller during this time. In 1927 he moved to Berlin where he participated in group exhibitions, including those organized by the Berlin Secession. He received an MA degree in 1928 from the State Institute of Higher Learning, Berlin, after which he became a teacher. He began photographing in 1933 when he made a contract with Presse-Photo, Berlin. In that year he moved to San Francisco where he worked as a press photographer for a number of German publications until 1936. In 1937 he began teaching at San Francisco State College. During these years he was active as a photographer and a painter. In 1973 he retired as a professor at San Francisco State University. He was awarded a Simon Guggenheim Fellowship in 1977 in recognition for his achievements in photography. He continues to be active as a painter and photographer in San Francisco.

ARVID GUTSCHOW Born 1900, Hamburg, Germany. As a self-taught photographer he financed his law studies during the years of inflation by selling his own photographs to magazines. Following his promotion he pursued the course of a high-ranking civil servant. He carried on with his photography merely as a sideline. His book of plates, *See, Sand, Sonne,* came out in Hamburg in 1930 and ranks among the style-creating photography books of modern times. His themes stem from his interests: the countryside, agriculture, and industry. He lives in Seebergen near Bremen.

HEINZ HAJEK-HALKE Born 1898, Berlin, Germany. In 1920 he began studying art with Emil Orlik at the Berliner Kunstgewerbemuseum. He subsequently became a newspaper illustrator, picture editor, and teacher at Charlottenburger Kunstgewerbeschule, where he first became seriously involved with photography as a means of creative expression. In the 1930s he turned to press photography for his livelihood. In the 1920s and 1930s he traveled extensively in Europe, from Lapland to Spain and overseas to the Azores and Brazil. During the 1930s he also did publicity photography for a Hamburg chemical-pharmaceutical firm and for the airplane manufacturer Dornier. After World War II he continued to do commercial photography. In 1955 he was appointed a lecturer in photography at the Hochschule für bildende Künste in Berlin-Charlottenburg. He is now retired and lives in Berlin.

RAOUL HAUSMANN Born 1886, Vienna, Austria. At the age of fourteen he went to Berlin to study art. In 1912 he began to write articles for *Der Sturm* and became deeply involved with the avant-garde movement in art. In 1918 he became a member of the Dada group in Berlin and began to make photomontages. During the 1920s he was involved with various subversive political and antiwar movements. In the early 1930s he began to work seriously with the camera as a means of expression. After 1933, the year he left Berlin for France, he photographed landscapes, close-up heads of people, and did studies of nudes in a straightforward fashion that was stylistically his own. In 1944 he settled in Limoges, France, where he died in 1971.

HEINRICH HEIDERSBERGER Born 1906, Ingolstadt, Germany. After going to school in Linz and studying architecture for three years in Graz, he took himself to Paris for two years in order to study painting and acquire a self-taught knowledge of photography. From 1936 he worked as a freelance photojournalist in Berlin. During World War II he managed the picture department of an armament business. After the war he became a self-employed photographer and since 1961 has had his own photographic studio in Schloss Wolfsburg. The main themes of his work are architecture and experimental photography. He lives in Wolfsburg.

FLORENCE HENRI Born 1895, New York City. She began studies in music in Berlin. By 1924 she had become primarily interested in art and studied in Paris with Léger and Ozenfant. In 1927 she was a student of Moholy-Nagy's and Joseph Albers's at the Bauhaus. At that time she began to work seriously with photography. In 1929 she returned to Paris, where she became a portrait and advertising photographer but still worked as an abstract painter and printmaker. Since 1963 she has lived at Bellival, France.

MARTA HOEPFFNER Born 1912, Pirmasens, Germany. Having studied painting, graphics, and photography under Willi Baumeister at the Frankfurt Kunstschule, she founded the Studio für Fotografik in Frankfurt in 1934. She concerned herself mainly with experimental photography, surrealistic photomontage, and photograms. Her studio was destroyed during the war in 1944. She moved to Hofheim/Taunus where in 1950 she opened a private school of photography. She continued her photographic experiments following the tradition of the Frankfurt Kunstschule and the Bauhaus: abstract »photographics,« »interference pictures,« and the first »color photograms« came into being and finally in 1966 the first »variochromatic light objects.« In 1971 Marta Hoepffner transferred her school to Kressbronn where she still works as a freelance artist.

EWALD HOINKIS Born 1897, Görlitz, Germany. He was self-taught as a photographer while a schoolboy. As an amateur he had his photographs published in such magazines as *Gartenlaube* and *UHU,* as well as the annual *Deutsches Lichtbild* in 1928/1929. He became a professional photographer in 1929, first in Görlitz and later in Berlin. He made picture stories, and his work was featured on the cover of Ullstein publications. In the mid-1930s he was a pioneer color photographer. In 1937 he was appointed a teacher at the Meisterschule für Grafik und Buchgewerbe in Leipzig. From 1949 to 1954 he was active as a professional photographer in Munich, then he moved to Frankfurt am Main. He died in Bühl/Baden in 1960.

LOTTE JACOBI Born 1896, Thorn, Germany. At the age of eight she began learning the techniques of photography from her father, a professional photographer whose studio was in Posen, a part of Germany before World War I. When she was twenty, she moved to Munich. In 1925 she attended the Bavarian State Academy of Photography (Bayerische Staatslehranstalt für Photographie). Her father established a studio in Berlin in 1920. After finishing her training in Munich, she moved to Berlin in 1927 and joined her father. In Berlin she practiced as a portrait photographer specializing in likenesses of stage and film personalities until 1935, when she moved to New York. In America she established a portrait studio and remained active in this field until the mid-1950s. In 1955 she moved to Deering, New Hampshire, where she has spent much of her time printing her negatives in preparation for exhibitions in the United States and Europe.

GYORGY KEPES Born 1906, Selyp, Hungary. He initially studied painting at the Academy of Fine Arts in Budapest but turned to work in motion pictures in 1929. At Moholy's invitation, in 1930 he moved to Berlin, where he was employed in still photography and motion picture work. In 1936 he followed Moholy to London and the next year moved to Chicago, where he became head of the light department of the New Bauhaus. In 1945 he joined the faculty of the School of Architecture of Massachusetts Institute of Technology in Cambridge to teach visual design courses. He has retired from teaching but is still active as a painter and photographer.

EDMUND KESTING Born 1892, Dresden, Germany. He studied art at the Kunstakademie in Dresden, 1911-1916. In 1920 he began photographing. After 1933 his work was restricted by the government, due to his ties with the avantgarde movement. In 1948 he was appointed a professor at the Hochschule für bildende und angewandte Kunst Berlin-Weissensee, and in 1955 he became a professor at the Deutsche Hochschule für Filmkunst in Dresden. He died in 1970 in Berlin.

ANNELIESE KRETSCHMER Born 1903, Dortmund, Germany. From 1920 to 1922 Kretschmer attended the Kunstgewerbeschule in Munich. From 1922 to 1924 she studied in Essen under L.V. Kaenel; with Franz Fiedler in Dresden from 1924 to 1928. She married Sigmund Kretschmer, a sculptor, in 1928 in Dresden. In 1934 they moved to Dortmund, where she opened a photography studio that remained active until 1975. She still lives in Dortmund.

HELMAR LERSKI   Born 1871, Strasbourg, France. In 1911 he began to photograph, using lighting techniques he had learned as a long-time professional actor. He learned much from his wife, who was a professional photographer. By 1914 he had established his personal style. In 1915 he returned to Europe (after spending 1893-1914 in the United States) and showed his portraits in a Berlin exhibition. This led to his career as a cameraman for a number of major films. He returned to portrait photography in 1929. In the 1930s he used his special type of photograph to record the Jewish and Near Eastern people. One of his most innovative works was a series of one hundred seventy-five portraits of one man, made in 1937–1938, called *Verwandlung durch Licht.* He died in Zurich in 1956.

ALICE LEX-NERLINGER   Born 1893, Berlin, Germany. Having completed her study of art under Emil Orlik at the Gewerbemuseum in Berlin, she worked as a freelance artist. In 1919 she married the painter Oscar Nerlinger and became a member of the group »Die Zeitgemässen.« In 1928 she joined the KPD and the ASSO (Association for the Revolutionary Creative Artists of Germany). In her work, which included photomontage and photograms, she became increasingly involved in politics. From 1933 she was politically persecuted by the Nazis and was forbidden to work. After World War II she worked as a freelance artist in East Berlin. She died in 1975 in East Berlin.

HERBERT LIST   Born 1903, Hamburg, Germany. After spending a number of years in the 1920s as a talented amateur and then receiving technical instruction from Andreas Feininger, he became a professional photographer in the early 1930s. In 1936 he left Germany and became a fashion photographer in London. Later he moved to Paris, where his photographs were reproduced in French magazines such as *Verve* and *Vogue.* His work also appeared in *Life* and *Harper's Bazaar.* He photographed extensively in Greece in the 1930s as well as from 1945 to 1946. From 1946 to 1962 he concentrated on portraits of prominent artists. He died in 1975 in Munich.

HEINZ LOEW   Born 1903, Leipzig, Germany. After graduating from the foundation course at the Bauhaus in Dessau he worked in collaboration with Oskar Schlemmer from 1926 through 1927 on the Bauhaus stage project. In 1927 he founded with Jost Schmidt the plastic workshop at the Bauhaus. In 1930, after organizing exhibitions and working on advertising design in Magdeburg, Leipzig, and Berlin, he founded »Studio Z« in Berlin. He emigrated to London in 1936. He is now living in Edgeware, England.

FELIX H. MAN   Born 1893, Freiburg, Breisgau, Germany. He studied art in Munich and Berlin, 1912-1914 and turned from being an illustrator to becoming a photographer in 1928. During 1928-1934 he had many photo-essays published in the *Münchner Illustrierte Presse* and the *Berliner Illustrirte Zeitung.* He moved to England in 1934, where in 1934-1936, under the name »Lensman«, he worked for the *Daily Mirror.* From 1938 to 1957 he was a photographer for the *London Picture Post, Time-Life,* and the London *Sunday Times.* He now divides his time between London and Rome, devoting himself to his large collection of lithography.

WERNER MANTZ   Born 1901, Cologne, Germany. During 1920-1921 he studied at the Bavarian State Academy for Photography in Munich. In 1921 he set up a photography studio in Cologne. In 1926 he began to concentrate on architectural photography. Among those who gave him commissions were the architects Riphan, Nöcher, Grod, and Schumacher and the city of Cologne. In 1932 he opened a studio in Maastricht, the Netherlands, where he settled in 1938. During 1937-1938 he did photodocumentation of mines in Holland. He now lives in Maastricht.

ELLI MARCUS   Born 1899, Berlin, Germany. Before she was twenty years of age and after a short apprenticeship, she set up a studio in Berlin and began specializing in stage photography. She was the first woman to do close-up portraits on stage during rehearsals, using existing lights. Her dramatic photographs of notable stage personalities were reproduced in popular periodicals and used for publicity purposes. She also did fashion and advertising photography. Like many Jewish photographers, she left Germany in 1933 and moved to Paris. When the Nazis took over Paris in 1941, she moved to New York City. In the United States she again established a photography studio and specialized in portraits of famous people in the arts. In 1956 she retired as a photographer. She died in New York in 1977.

LUCIA MOHOLY (née Schultz)   Born 1900, Prague, Czechoslovakia. She studied philosophy and art history in Prague then in 1920 went to Berlin. She married László Moholy-Nagy in 1921. To aid him in his work with photography, she learned photographic techniques at the Akademie für graphische Künste und Buchgewerbe in Leipzig. She was also an independent photographer of architecture and people during the late 1920s, when she lived at the Bauhaus. From 1929 to 1932 she taught at the Johannes-Itten-Schule in Berlin. With the coming of the Nazis she moved to Paris in 1933. In 1934 she moved to London. There she taught photography at the London School of Printing and Graphic Arts and the Central School of Arts and Crafts, and wrote a history of photography from 1839 to 1939. She now lives in Zurich.

LÁSZLÓ MOHOLY-NAGY Born 1895, Bacsbarsod, Hungary. While recovering from war wounds in World War I, he became interested in art. He became a painter and made contact with avant-garde artists in Budapest in 1918. The following year he went to Vienna and to Berlin. There he became associated with the *Der Sturm* group.

In 1922 he participated in the International Dada-Constructivist Congress in Weimar. In 1922 he began experimenting with photographs in collaboration with his wife, Lucia Schultz, whom he had married the previous year. He was appointed a master at the Bauhaus in 1923. In 1926 he did his first film, *Berliner Stilleben.* In 1928 he left the Bauhaus and moved to Berlin, where he did designs for advertising theater and opera. He moved to Amsterdam in 1934 and to London in 1935, where he did designs for advertising and a series of documentary photographs of the markets of the city.

In 1937 he moved to Chicago and founded the New Bauhaus School of Design, out of which grew a part of the Institute of Design of Illinois Institute of Technology. He died in Chicago in 1946.

GEORG MUCHE Born 1895, Querfurt, Germany. From 1916 through 1920 he belonged as painter, craftsman, and architect to the avant-garde Berlin group of artists »Der Sturm.« Subsequently, until 1927 he taught textile design at the Bauhaus in Weimar and Dessau. In 1931 he accepted the chair as professor at the Kunstakademie in Breslau. He had to retire from there in 1933. From 1939 through 1959 he taught at the Textilschule in Krefeld. Ever since his time at the Bauhaus, Muche has taken an interest in experimental photography and problems relating to photographic theories. He now lives in Lindau-Schachen.

MARTIN MUNKACSI (Marmorstein) Born 1896, Kolozsvar, Hungary (now Cluj, Roumania). He was self-trained as a photographer. By 1923 he was doing news photography for a Budapest daily sports journal, *Az Est.* He moved to Berlin in 1927 to work for Ullstein Press's publications, *Biz* and *Die Dame,* as well as general interest periodicals such as *Berliner Illustrirte Zeitung.* He left Germany in 1934 to become the chief fashion photographer for *Harper's Bazaar* in New York. He also did photography for *Town & Country, Good Housekeeping,* and *Ladies' Home Journal.* He died in 1963 in New York.

WALTER PETERHANS Born 1897, Frankfurt am Main, Germany. His father was the director of Zeiss Ikon, Dresden. In 1920-1921 he studied at the Technical College in Munich and in 1921-1923 studied mathematics, philosophy, and art history at Göttingen University. During 1925-1926 he studied techniques of reproduction at the State Academy of Printing and Graphic Art in Leipzig, taking his degree in photography at Weimar. In 1927-1929 he had a studio in Berlin and also gave private lessons in photography to some pupils, among them Ellen Auerbach and Grete Stern. From 1929 to 1932 he was the head of photography at the Bauhaus, Dessau. In 1932 he moved to Berlin, where he had a teaching post at Mies van der Rohe's private institute until 1933. For the next two years he taught at the Reimann-Häring-School in Berlin. During 1935-1937 he was a freelance photographer in Berlin, taking commissions from industrial concerns. In 1938 he moved to the United States, where he had a professorship in the department of architecture at the Illinois Institute of Technology in Chicago. He taught visual fundamentals and art history. In 1953 he was guest lecturer at the Hochschule für Gestaltung in Ulm and in 1959-1960 guest professor at the Academy of Fine Arts, Hamburg. He died in 1960 in Stetten, Baden-Württemberg.

ROBERT PETSCHOW Born 1888, Kolberg/Pommern, Germany. While studying to be an engineer, he became interested in ballooning. He took up photography to record the scenes he observed as he floated over the countryside. He joined the German air service to continue his activities as a balloonist. After World War I his interest in ballooning continued, as did his interest in aerial photography, for which he became very well known. He died in Haldensleben in 1945.

ALBERT RENGER-PATZSCH Born 1897, Würzburg, Germany. At the Dresden Technische Hochschule, he emphasized the study of chemistry. In 1922 he became the director of the picture department of the Folkwang Archive and the Auriga Verlag. He moved to Bad Harzburg in 1925 and established a studio. He went to Essen in 1928, where in 1933 he became a teacher of photography at the Folkwangschule. After 1944 he lived in Wamel near Soest, where he devoted much time to landscape photography. It was in Wamel that he died in 1966.

HANS RICHTER Born 1888, Berlin, Germany. Richter attended the Berliner Hochschule für Bildende Kunst in 1908 and the Weimarer Akademie in 1909. In 1916 he joined the Zurich dada group. In 1920 he made his first attempts at motion pictures, and *Rhythmus 21* was his first film, followed by *Inflation* (1928) *Vormittagsspuk,* and *Rennsymphonie* (1929). Richter worked in the U.S.S.R. (1931) before emigrating to Switzerland in 1933. In 1941 he founded the Film Institute at New York's City College. Among his other films are *Dreams That Money Can Buy* (1944-1947), *8 x 8,* and *Dadascope.* He died in Locarno, Switzerland, in 1976.

FRANZ ROH Born 1890, Apolda/Thüringen, Germany. In 1918, following the completion of his studies in literature and history of art at the universities of Leipzig, Berlin, Basel, and Munich, he became assistant to Heinrich Wölfflin. From 1919 he was on the staff of the magazines *Cicerone* and *Das Kunstblatt*. His book, *Nachexpressionismus – Magischer Realismus,* came out in 1925. In 1929, in collaboration with Jan Tschichold, he published *Foto-Auge*. This was the first publication on experimental artistic photography. After the war he became professor of modern art history at the University of Munich and worked as an editor and art critic. In 1954 he founded the Gesellschaft der Freunde junger Kunst (Society for the Friends of Modern Art) of which he was president until 1964. He died in 1965 in Munich.

WERNER ROHDE Born 1906, Bremen, Germany. He began the study of painting in 1925 at Burg Giebichenstein Kunstgewerbeschule near Halle. There he met Hans Finsler, who encouraged him to continue with photography as well as painting. He also met Moholy in Halle. While continuing to paint, he became a portrait, fashion, and advertising photographer. In 1929 and 1930 he was in Paris, where he met and became a close friend of Paul Citroen. In 1931 he returned to Bremen, where he continued as a photographer and painter. He now lives near Bremen.

ERICH SALOMON Born 1886, Berlin, Germany. He studied mechanical engineering and law at the University of Munich, from which he received a doctoral degree. After World War I, during which he was a prisoner of the French for four years, he was employed by the publicity department of Ullstein Verlag. In 1927 he acquired an Ermanox camera and decided to make photojournalism his profession, specializing in candid pictures of diplomats and heads of state taken in unposed situations. He became a major contributor to *Berliner Illustrirte Zeitung* and other mass-circulation picture periodicals. He died in 1944 in a German concentration camp.

AUGUST SANDER Born 1876, Herdorf, Germany. He worked as an assistant for a number of photographers until 1910, when he established his own studio in Cologne. In 1918 he became acquainted with the painter Franz Wilhelm Seiwert, who urged him to undertake a sociological study of the German people by taking their portraits. This project became »Man of the 20th Century.« With unretouched portraits he sought to reveal every detail of his subject. In 1929 he published with *Antlitz der Zeit* the first phase of this vast undertaking. After 1934 the book was banned, and the plates from which it had been printed were confiscated.

While still maintaining his studio and taking portraits, he devoted more time to landscape photography. With the help of his son, Günther, the Sander studio continued to operate after World War II, but August did little photography, concentrating instead on making prints from older negatives. He died in 1964 in Cologne.

CHRISTIAN SCHAD Born 1894, Miesbach, Oberbayern, Germany. He began the study of art at the Kunstakademie in Munich in 1913. From 1915 through 1920 he was associated with the Dada movement in Zurich, and in 1918 he began to make his cameraless photographic images that were called »Schadographs«. In the 1920s he was primarily involved with painting in the Neue Sachlichkeit style. He continued as a painter from the 1930s to the present, returning to the production of »Schadographs« in 1973. He died in 1982 in Keilberg, Spessart.

FRIEDRICH SEIDENSTÜCKER Born 1882, Unna, Germany. In 1904 he moved to Berlin and became a student at the Technische Hochschule. There he began modeling animals. To provide study pictures, he took up the camera to record the appearance of animals at the Berliner Zoo. During the period 1919-1922 he studied art and became an exhibiting sculptor of animals, while freelancing as a photographer to make a living. He was successful as a photographer but not as a sculptor. His photographs were widely reproduced in such publications as *Berliner Illustrirte Zeitung, Die Neue Linie, Die Dame, and Der Querschnitt* and were included in the annuals of *Das deutsche Lichtbild* and *Arts et Métiers Graphiques.* He continued to photograph into the 1950s and died in Berlin in 1966.

ANTON STANKOWSKI Born 1906, Gelsenkirchen, Germany. During the years 1927-1929 he studied photography and design with Max Burchartz at the Folkwangschule in Essen. For the next eight years he worked as a graphic designer and photographer and painted in Zurich. In 1937 he moved to Stuttgart, where his interest in photography for himself and for advertising clients continued. At this time he also carried out graphic-design assignments. He continued to be active as a photographer after World War II. He lives in Stuttgart.

GRETE STERN Born 1904, Wuppertal-Elberfeld, Germany. During the period 1925-1927 she studied art with H.E. Schneidler at the Kunstgewerbeschule in Stuttgart. In 1927 she moved to Berlin and began two years of study in photography as a private pupil of Walter Peterhans. She studied further with Peterhans at the Bauhaus in Dessau in 1930 and 1931. With Ellen Auerbach she founded the studio of Ringl & Pit in 1930 in Berlin. In 1933 she moved to London, where she did portraits and engaged in photopropaganda production. She next moved to Buenos Aires, where she established herself as a portrait, still-life, and landscape photographer. She continues to live in Buenos Aires.

SASHA STONE   Born in Russia. As a youth he was taken to New York City, where he learned technical drafting. In Paris he studied drawing and sculpture and became a photographer to earn a living. From Paris he moved to Berlin, where he established a professional photography studio to serve advertising agencies and architects. In 1933 he moved to Brussels. No record has been found, but it appears that he died around 1944 in a German concentration camp.

STUDIO RINGL & PIT   See Grete Stern

UMBO (Otto Umbehr)   Born 1902, Düsseldorf, Germany. Initially, his interest in the arts was focused on acting, ceramics, and printmaking. During the period 1921-1923 he studied at the Bauhaus. In 1923 he moved to Berlin, where among other things he worked on the film *Berlin–Symphonie einer Grosstadt.* From 1928 to 1933 he worked with the Berlin photography agency, Dephot. When Dephot closed in 1933, he became a full-time freelance photojournalist. He then served in the German army. After World War II he moved to Hannover, where again he was a photojournalist. He died in Hannover in 1980.

KLAUS WITTKUGEL   Born 1910, Kiel, Germany. From 1929 through 1932 he attended the Folkwangschule in Essen, followed by a year at the Abendschule an der Meisterschule für Graphik und Buchkunst in Berlin. After World War II he was active as a graphic designer and taught at the Hochschule für bildende und angewandte Kunst Berlin-Weissensee. In 1952 he was appointed a professor at the Kunsthochschule in Berlin, where he presently lives.

YVA (Else Simon)   Born 1900, Berlin, Germany. As a fashion and portrait photographer she established a studio in Berlin. In 1936, being Jewish, she was forced to give up the management of her studio but continued as a photographer. After 1938, no longer allowed to be a photographer, she became an x-ray technician. She was sent to a concentration camp, where she died in 1942.

WILLY OTTO ZIELKE   Born 1902, Lodz, Poland. He studied railway engineering in Tashkent, Russia, until his family returned to Germany and settled in Munich. There he began his studies of photography at the Bayerische Staatslehranstalt für Fotografie, where, in 1928, he was appointed master teacher. In 1932, Zielke started working with motion pictures, and his first film, *Arbeitslos,* earned him the commission of Das Stahltier (forbidden in 1935 by national socialist film censorship). In 1936, Zielke was producer for the prologue to Leni Riefenstahl's film *Olympiad.* After 1945 he worked as a translator in Potsdam, and returned to West Germany in 1951, working as an industrial filmmaker (at times under the pseudonym Victor Valet). He now lives in Bad Pyrmont, Germany.

A SELECTED CHRONOLOGY

1910   August Sander establishes a portrait studio in Cologne.

1911   Helmar Lerski begins photographing.

1915   Lerski's first exhibition of his portraits in Germany; he turns from still photography to motion picture photography in Berlin.

1918   Christian Schad makes his first Schadographs.
Elli Marcus opens a portrait studio in Berlin.

1919   Werner Mantz begins two years of study of photography at the Bayerische Staatslehranstalt für Photographie in Munich.
The Bauhaus is founded in Weimar.
Lázsló Moholy-Nagy comes to Berlin from Vienna.

1920   Anneliese Kretschmer begins two years of study of photography at the Kunstgewerbeschule in Munich.

1921   Edmund Kesting begins photographing.
Moholy and Lucia Schultz are married.
Herbert Bayer enrolls at the Bauhaus.
Mantz establishes a studio in Cologne.

1922   Moholy participates in the dada-constructivist congress held in Weimar.
Kretschmer begins two years of study of photography with L.V. Kaenel in Essen.
Aenne Biermann begins photographing.
Albert Renger-Patzsch becomes director of the Bildstelle of the Folkwang archives.
Paul Citroen begins a period of study at the Bauhaus.

1923   Martin Munkacsi begins taking news photographs for a Budapest newspaper.
Moholy is appointed a master at the Bauhaus.

1924   Kretschmer begins four years of study of photography with Franz Fiedler in Dresden.

1925   The Leica camera is introduced at the Leipzig trade fair.
Walter Peterhans begins two years of study of reproductive techniques at Staatliche Akademie für Graphik und Buchgewerbe in Leipzig.
Herbert Bayer is appointed a master at the Bauhaus to teach typography and advertising layout.
The Bauhaus is moved from Weimar to Dessau.
Moholy's *Malerei, Fotografie, Film* is published.
Renger-Patzsch establishes a studio in Bad Harzburg.
Citroen begins photographing.
Renger-Patzsch's first book of photographs, *Das Chorgestühl von Cappenberg,* is published.
Anton Stankowski begins two years of study with Max Burchartz at the Folkwangschule in Essen.

1926   Karl Blossfeldt's detailed photographs of plants are first published.
Umbo works as a portrait photographer in Berlin.
Hans Finsler begins teaching photography at the Burg Giebichenstein near Halle.
Burchartz is appointed a professor at the Folkwangschule to teach graphic design, photography, and the theory of advertising.
W. M. Heinz Loew begins four years of study at the Bauhaus.

1927   Florence Henri attends classes at the Bauhaus.
Munkacsi arrives in Berlin and is employed by Ullstein Verlag.
The photography yearbook *Das deutsche Lichtbild* is first published.
Renger-Patzsch's book *Die Halligen* is published.
Werner Rohde begins photographing.
Mantz begins photographing architecture.
Raoul Hausmann becomes seriously involved with photography.
Grete Stern studies photography with Peterhans as a private student.
Alfred Ehrhardt begins a period of study at the Bauhaus.

1928 Umbo works as a cinematographer on Walter Ruttman's film, *Berlin–Symphonie einer Grossstadt.*

Henri's photographs are published in Amsterdam in *i10,* with an introduction by Moholy.

Moholy leaves the Bauhaus and moves to Berlin.

The »Neue Wege der Photographie« exhibition is held in Jena.

Felix Man turns from being an illustrator to doing photography for *Münchner Illustrierte Presse* and *Berliner Illustrirte Zeitung.*

Simon Guttmann and Alfred Marks establish the photography picture agency Dephot.

Blossfeldt's book *Urformen der Kunst* is published.

Renger-Patzsch has his book *Die Welt ist schön* published.

1929 International »Film und Foto« exhibition takes place in Stuttgart.

Tim Gidal begins his career as a photojournalist.

Ewald Hoinkis leaves the field of industrial administration to become a professional photographer and graphic designer.

Peterhans is appointed a master at the Bauhaus to teach photography and graphic design.

Lerski returns to still photography after being a cinematographer since 1915.

Rohde begins two years of painting and photographing in Paris, where he meets and becomes a close friend of Citroen.

Sander's *Antlitz der Zeit* is published.

Lucia Moholy begins teaching photography in Berlin at Itten's School of Art.

Werner Gräff's *Es kommt der neue Fotograf* is published.

»Fotografie der Gegenwart« exhibition is held in Essen.

Marianne Breslauer begins photographing.

Marta Hoepffner begins the study of design and photography with Willi Baumeister.

1930 Biermann's book *60 Fotos* is published.

Gyorgy Kepes comes to Berlin from Budapest.

»Das Lichtbild« exhibition is held in Munich.

Franz Roh's and Jan Tschichold's book *Foto-Auge/Œil et Photo/Photo-Eye* is published.

Roh's book *Moholy-Nagy–60 Fotos* is published.

Seidenstücker becomes a full-time photographer working for Ullstein Verlag.

Ringl & Pit studio is opened in Berlin by Grete Stern and Ellen Auerbach.

Arvid Gutschow's book *See, Sand, Sonne* is published.

1931 »Das Lichtbild«—the second exhibition with this title—is held in Essen.

Walter Benjamin's *Kleine Geschichte der Photographie* is published.

Lerski's book *Köpfe des Alltags* is published.

Erich Salomon's book *Berühmte Zeitgenossen in unbewachten Augenblicken* is published.

1932 Herbert Bayer begins to work seriously with photography.

Blossfeldt's book *Wundergarten der Natur* is published.

Munkacsi flies to Brazil by Zeppelin and does major photographic essay on coffee.

Man leaves Germany and begins photojournalistic work in London.

Mantz leaves Germany for the Netherlands.

Peterhans moves to Berlin, where he combines teaching photography with assignments for industrial and advertising clients.

Finsler establishes a department of photography at the Zurich Kunstgewerbeschule.

The Bauhaus is moved to Berlin.

Blossfeldt dies.

Willy Zielke photographs the innovative film *Arbeitslos.*

1933 Andreas Feininger moves to Sweden.

Renger-Patzsch begins teaching at the Folkwangschule.

Burchartz is dismissed as a professor at the Folkwangschule and his work is declared as being »degenerate« by the Nazis.

He establishes a private studio, where he carries on as a photographer and graphic designer until he enters the army in 1939.

Stern moves to London.

Elli Marcus moves to Paris.

The Bauhaus is closed.

Biermann dies.

Auerbach moves to Palestine.

Loew moves to London.

Kesting prevented from photographing by Nazis, who consider his work »degenerate«.

1934 Hans Bellmer's photographs of his large doll are published in *Minotaure.*

Moholy moves to Amsterdam.

Munkacsi leaves Germany for the United States, where he is employed by *Harper's Bazaar* to do fashion photography.

Kretschmer establishes a studio in Dortmund.

Lucia Moholy moves to London.

Hoepffner establishes a studio in Frankfurt.

1935   Moholy moves to London.
       Jacobi moves to New York.

1936   A second »Film und Foto« exhibition (all German) is
       held in Düsseldorf.
       Gidal moves to Palestine.
       Herbert List moves to London.
       Stern goes to Buenos Aires and marries Horacio
       Coppola.
       Auerbach moves to the United States.

1937   Moholy moves to Chicago and founds the New
       Bauhaus.
       Bellmer creates a second doll, which he photo-
       graphs extensively.
       Stankowski moves to Stuttgart.
       Ehrhardt's book Das Watt is published.

1938   Peterhans moves to Chicago to teach in the
       architecture department of the Institute of Design.
       Irene and Herbert Bayer leave Germany for the
       United States.

A SELECTED BIBLIOGRAPHY

Books, catalogs, and articles on avant-garde photography in Germany from 1919-1939

I *GENERAL*

Bertonati, Emilio. *Das Experimentelle Photo in Deutschland, 1918-1940.* Munich: Galleria del Levante, 1978.

Eskildsen, Ute; Schmalriede, Manfred; Horak, Jan-Christopher. *Film und Foto der zwanziger Jahre.* Stuttgart: Verlag Gerd Hatje, 1979.

Gidal, Tim. *Deutschland, Beginn des modernen Photojournalismus.* Lucerne and Frankfurt: C.J. Bucher, 1972.

Graff, von Werner. *Es kommt der neue Fotograf!* Cologne: Verlag Hermann Reckendorf, 1978.

Lohse, Bernd. »Photo-Journalism, The Legendary Twenties,« *Camera,* April 1967.

Mellor, David, ed. *Germany, The New Photography 1927-1933.* London: Arts Council of Great Britain, 1978.

Molderings, Herbert. »Überlegungen zur Fotografie der Neuen Sachlichkeit und der Bauhäuser,« *Kritische Berichte* IV, 2/3, 1977.

——. *La Photographie sous la République de Weimar.* Stuttgart: L'Institut pour les Relations Culturelles avec l'Etranger, 1979.

Porter, Allan. »Camera Eye: Fascination and Imagination,« *Camera,* October 1979.

Roh, Franz. »The Independents, Mechanism and Expression/The Essence and Value of Photography,« *Camera,* April 1967.

Roh, Franz, and Tschichold, Jan, eds. *Foto-Auge, Œil et photo, Photo-Eye.* New York: Arno Press, 1973.

Schöppe, Wilhelm. *Meister der Kamera erzählen.* Halle, Saale: 1936.

Steinorth, Karl. »The International Werkbund-Exhibition 'Film und Foto', Stuttgart, 1929.« *Camera,* October 1979.

II *BIOGRAPHIES*

Avedon, Richard. »Munkacsi,« *Harper's Bazaar,* June 1964.

Baum, Timothy. »Hans Bellmer,« *Photo Bulletin.* Los Angeles: G. Ray Hawkins Gallery, December 1981.

Beck, Tom. *Lotte Jacobi: Portraits and Photogenics.* Baltimore: University of Maryland Press and Baltimore County Library, 1978.

Clary, Max. »Eugène Carrière de la Photographie: Munkacsi,« *Le Miroir du Monde,* October 1933.

Erikson, Erik; Arnheim, Rudolf; Goeritz, Matthias; Piene, Otto. *Gyorgy Kepes: Works in Review.* Boston: Museum of Science, 1973.

Gernsheim, Helmut. »Photographs by Felix H. Man,« *Creative Camera,* July 1972.

Hackett, Gabriel. P. »Martin Munkacsi,« *Infinity,* September 1963.

Haenlein, Carl. *Raoul Hausmann: Retrospektive.* Hannover: Kestner-Gesellschaft, 1981.

Haus, Andreas. *Raoul Hausmann, Kamerafotografien 1927-1957.* Munich: Schirmer/Mosel, 1979.

——. *Photographs & Photograms: Moholy-Nagy.* London: Thames and Hudson, and New York: Pantheon Books, 1980.

Haz, Nicholas. »Martin Munkacsi,« *Camera Craft,* July 1935.

Honnef, Klaus. *Albert Renger-Patzsch: Fotografien 1925-1960.* Bonn: Rheinisches Landesmuseum, 1977.

——. *Karl Blossfeldt: Fotografien 1900-1932.* Bonn: Rheinisches Landesmuseum, 1977.

——. *Werner Mantz: Fotografien 1926-1938.* Bonn: Rheinisches Landesmuseum, 1978.

Humphrey, John. *As I (John Gutmann) Saw It.* San Francisco: San Francisco Museum of Modern Art, 1976.

Karia, Bhupendra. *Andreas Feininger.* New York: International Center of Photography, 1976.

Keller, Ulrich. *August Sander – Menschen des 20. Jahrhunderts: Portraitphotographien 1892-1952.* Edited by Gunther Sander. Munich: Schirmer/Mosel, 1980.

Kempe, Fritz. *Albert Renger-Patzsch: Der Fotograf der Dinge.* Essen: Ruhrland-und Heimat-Museum, 1967.

——. »Albert Renger-Patzsch (1867-1966): His Life and Personality.« *Camera,* April 1967.

Kohmen, Volker. *Ernst Fuhrmann.* Cologne: Galerie Rudolf Kicken, 1979.

Kramer, Robert. *August Sander: Photographs of an Epoch 1904-1959.* Millerton, NY: Aperture, 1980.

Lemagny, Jean-Claude, and Hopkinson, Tom. *Felix H. Man: 60 Ans de Photographie.* Paris: Goethe Institut, 1981.

Lerski, Anneliese. *Der Mensch, mein Bruder.* Dresden: Verlag der Kunst, 1958.

Lohse, Bernd. »Tim N. Gidal,« *Camera,* January 1975.

Lyon, Mark. »The Trees of Germany« (by Albert Renger-Patzsch). New York and Paris: *Zabriskie Photography Newsletter.* Fall 1980.

Marcenaro, Giuseppe, and Martini, Giovanni Battista. *Florence Henri, Aspetti di un Percorso 1910-1940.* Genoa: Sagep Editrice, 1979.

Marks, Robert W. »Portrait of Munkacsi,« *Coronet,* January 1940.

Metken, Günter. *Herbert List: Photographien 1930-1970.* New York: Rizzoli, 1976.

Moholy-Nagy, Sybil. *Moholy-Nagy, A Biography.* Introduction by Walter Gropius. New York: Harper & Bros., 1950.

Newhall, Beaumont, and Rice, Lee. *Herbert Bayer: Photographic Works.* Los Angeles: Arco Center for Visual Arts, 1977.

Osman, Colin. *Spontaneity & Style: Munkacsi.* New York: International Center of Photography, 1978.

Reinhardt, Georg. *Umbo: Photographien 1925-1933.* Hannover: Spectrum Photogalerie, 1979.

Rice, Leland R., and Steadman, David W., eds. *Photographs of Moholy-Nagy from the Collection of William Larson.* Claremont, CA.: The Galleries of the Claremont Colleges, 1975.

Roh, Franz. *Aenne Biermann.* Berlin: Klinkhardt & Biermann, 1930.

——. *L. Moholy-Nagy 60 Fotos.* Berlin: Klinkhardt & Biermann, 1930.

Roters, Eberhard. *Heinz Hajek-Halke: Fotografie, Foto-Grafik, Licht-Grafik.* Berlin: Galerie Werner Kunze, 1978.

Schurmann, Wilhelm. »Werner Mantz,« *Camera,* January 1977.

Schwartz, Arturo. *Dada Schad Dada.* Milan: Galleria Schwarz, 1971.

Turner, Peter. »Tim Gidal,« *Creative Camera,* May 1979.

Wilde, Jürgen, ed. *Frederick Seidenstücker: Von Weimar bis zum Ende–Fotografien aus bewegter Zeit.* Dortmund: Harenberg Kommunications, 1980.

Wingler, H.M. *Begegnungen mit Menschen: Das Fotografische Werk von Grete Stern.* Berlin: Bauhaus Archiv, 1975.

Wise, Kelley, ed. *Lotte Jacobi.* New York: Addison House, 1978.

III *BY THE PHOTOGRAPHERS*

Blossfeldt, Karl. *Art Forms in Nature.* New York: Weyhe, 1925.

Breslauer, Marianne. *Retrospektive Fotografie.* Bielefeld/Düsseldorf: Edition Marzona, 1979.

Citroen, Paul. *Retrospektive Fotografie.* Bielefeld/Düsseldorf: Edition Marzona, 1978.

Ehrhardt, Alfred. *Das Watt.* Forward by Dr. Kurt Dingelstedt. Hamburg: Ellermann Verlag, 1937.

———. *Muscheln und Schnecken.* Hamburg: Ellermann Verlag, 1941.

———. *Wattenmeer, Formen und Strukturen.* Munich: Starczewski Verlag, 1967.

Feininger, Andreas. *New Paths in Photography.* Boston: American Photographic Publishing Co., 1939.

Feininger, T. Lux. *Photographs of the Twenties and Thirties.* New York: Prakapas Gallery, 1980.

Finsler, Hans. *Mein Weg zur Fotografie–My Way to Photography.* Zurich: Pendo-Verlag, 1971.

Fuhrmann, Ernst. *Die Pflanze als Lebewesen.* Frankfurt: Societats Verlag, 1930.

———. *Hein Gorny.* Hannover: Spectrum Photogalerie, 1972.

Gutschow, Arvid. *See, Sand, Sonne.* Forward by Hans Leip. Hamburg: Gebr. Enoch Verlag, 1930.

Hajek-Halke, H. *Experimentelle Fotografie.* Bonn: Athenäum Verlag, 1955.

Henri, Florence. *Aspekte der Photographie der 20er Jahre.* Münster: Westfälischer Kunstverein, 1976.

Kepes, Gyorgy. *The New Landscape in Art and Sciences.* Chicago: P. Theobald, 1956.

Lerski, Helmar. *Köpfe des Alltags.* Berlin: Hermann Reckendorf Verlag, 1931.

Lex-Nerlinger, Alice. *Oskar Nerlinger.* Berlin: Akademie der Künste der DDR, 1975.

Man, Felix H. *Felix H. Man, 60 Jahre Fotografie.* Bielefeld: Kunsthalle Bielefeld, 1978.

Moholy, Lucia. *Marginalien zu Moholy-Nagy–Marginal Notes.* Krefeld: Scherpe Verlag, 1972.

Moholy-Nagy, László. *Malerei, Fotografie, Film.* Cambridge, Mass.: MIT Press, 1969.

———. *László Moholy-Nagy.* Stuttgart: Württembergischer Kunstverein, 1974.

———. *The New Vision.* New York: W.W. Norton, 1938.

———. *Vision in Motion.* Theobald Publishers, 1947.

Peterhans, Walter. »Zum gegenwärtigen Stand der Fotografie,« *Red D 5.* Prag, 1930.

Renger-Patzsch, Albert. *Das Chorgestühl von Cappenberg.* Essen: Folkwang Auriga, 1925.

———. *Die Welt ist schön.* Munich: Kurt Wolff, 1928.

———. *Eisen und Stahl.* Berlin: Hermann Reckendorf Verlag, 1931.

Salomon, Erich. *Berühmte Zeitgenossen in unbewachten Augenblicken.* Stuttgart: J. Engelhorn Nachf., 1931.

———. *Portrait einer Epoche.* New York: Macmillan, 1963.

Sander, August. *Antlitz der Zeit. 60 Fotos Deutscher Menschen.* Munich: Transmare-Kurt Wolff, 1929.

———. *Menschen ohne Maske.* Lucerne and Frankfurt: C.J. Bucher, 1971.

1 Erich Salomon, »Le voilà!«, Paris 1931

2   Erich Salomon, Politicians at Dinner, n.d.

3   Erich Salomon, A Press Ball, n.d.

4   Felix H. Man, Beercellar, Munich 1929

5   Tim Gidal, Beergarden, Munich 1929

6   Florence Henri, Portrait, ca. 1928

7   Raoul Hausmann, »Etude d'Expression«, 1931

8   Lotte Jacobi, Portrait Franz Lederer, ca. 1929

9   Helmar Lerski, Portrait, ca. 1930

10   Lucia Moholy, Portrait Georg Muche, 1927

11   August Sander, *Wife of the Painter Peter Abelen, Cologne 1926*

12 August Sander, College Graduate, 1926

13   Edmund Kesting, Self-portrait, ca. 1930

14   Lux Feininger, Portrait Clemens Röseler, n.d.

15   Irene Bayer, Portrait Study, 1928

16   Marianne Breslauer, Portrait Paul Citroen, ca. 1927

17   Lotte Jacobi, Portrait Käthe Kollwitz, n.d.

18   Raoul Hausmann, Self-portrait, Baltic Sea 1931

19   Paul Citroen, Double Portrait, ca. 1930

20　László Moholy-Nagy, Multiple Portrait, 1927

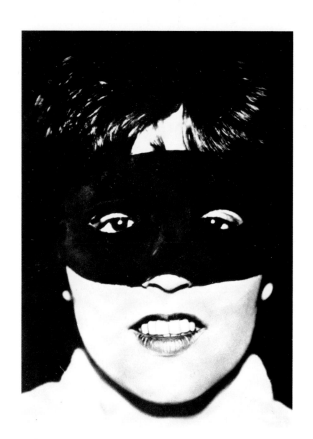 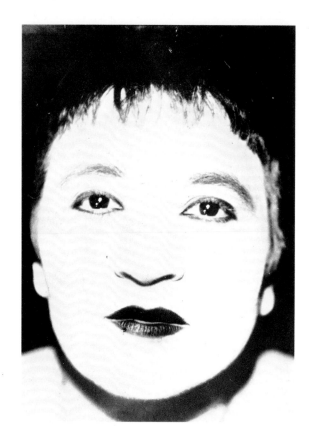

21/22   Umbo, Portraits, 1927/28

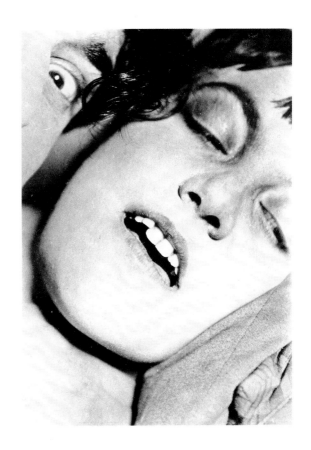
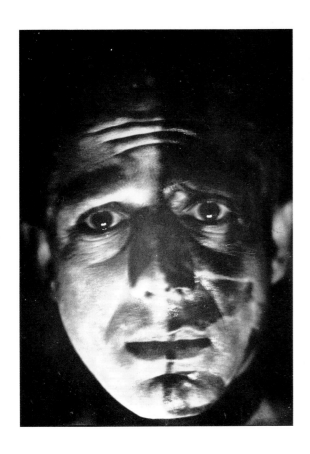
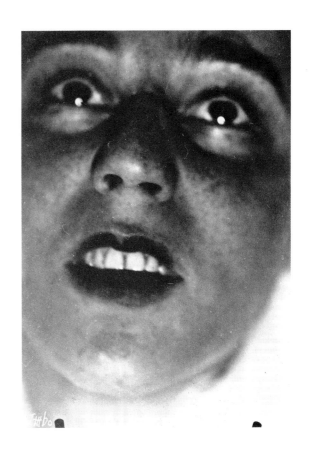

23   Max Burchartz, »Lotte's Eye«, ca. 1928

24   Tim Gidal, Self-portrait, 1930

25   Lucia Moholy, Portrait Franz Roh, 1926

26 Edmund Kesting, Portrait Ruth Poelzig, 1928

27   Raoul Hausmann, »Look«, 1930/31

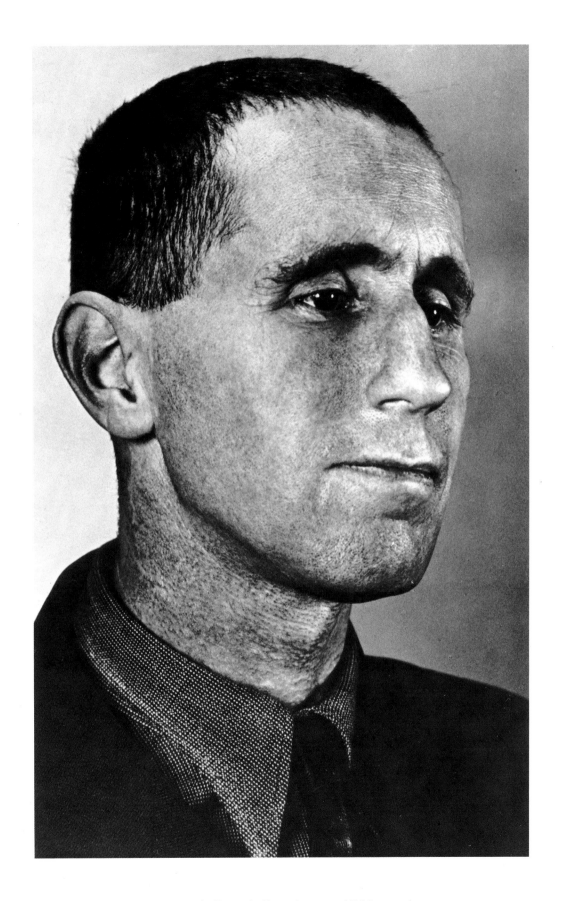

28   Grete Stern, Portrait Bertolt Brecht, ca. 1933

29   Lux Feininger, Untitled, ca. 1929

30   Heinz Loew, Untitled, 1927

31   Gyorgy Kepes, Untitled, 1930

32   John Gutmann, Untitled, Berlin 1933

33   László Moholy-Nagy, Street, Berlin 1928

34   Martin Munkacsi, Nice, 1931

35   Anton Stankowski, »Salutation«, Zurich 1932

36   Heinrich Heidersberger, Street Scene, n.d.

37   Umbo, Untitled, 1928

38   László Moholy-Nagy, From the Radio Tower Berlin, 1928

39   Martin Munkacsi, Street Scene, n.d.

40   Gyorgy Kepes, Untitled, 1930

41   Friedrich Seidenstücker, House Painters, 1928

42 Friedrich Seidenstücker, »Pfützenspringerin«, 1925

43   Martin Munkacsi, Children, Kissingen 1929

44   Martin Munkacsi, »Crowd«, ca. 1930

45   Anton Stankowski, »Zeitprotokoll mit Auto«, 1929

46   Anneliese Kretschmer, Untitled, Paris 1928

47   Anton Stankowski, »1/100 sec. at 70 km/h«, 1930

48   Werner Mantz, »Pressa«, Cologne 1928

49   Werner Mantz, »ADA«, 1930

50   Lucia Moholy, Bauhaus Dessau – Workshop Building, 1926

51   László Moholy-Nagy, Bauhaus Balconies, 1926

52   László Moholy-Nagy, Bauhaus Balconies, 1926

53   Albert Renger-Patzsch, Stairwell, 1929

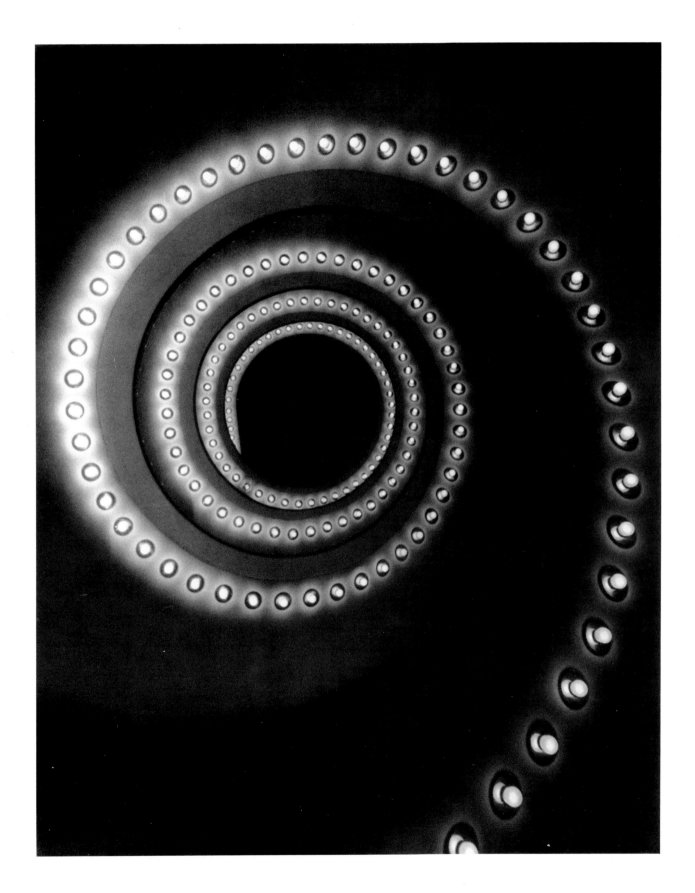

54   Studio August Sander, Spiral Light Bulbs, ca. 1930

55 Studio Ringl & Pit, »Pétrole Hahn«, 1928

56   Albert Renger-Patzsch, »Kaffee Hag«, Bremen 1925

57   Hans Finsler, »Sarizol«, ca. 1930

58   Studio Ringl & Pit, »Komol«, ca. 1931

59   Hans Finsler, Ceramic Tubing, ca. 1929

60   Ewald Hoinkis, Glasses, ca. 1927

61   Werner David Feist, »Electrola«, n.d.

62   Yva, Untitled, ca. 1928

63   Hans Finsler, Untitled, n.d.

64   Werner Rohde, Jewelry, 1930

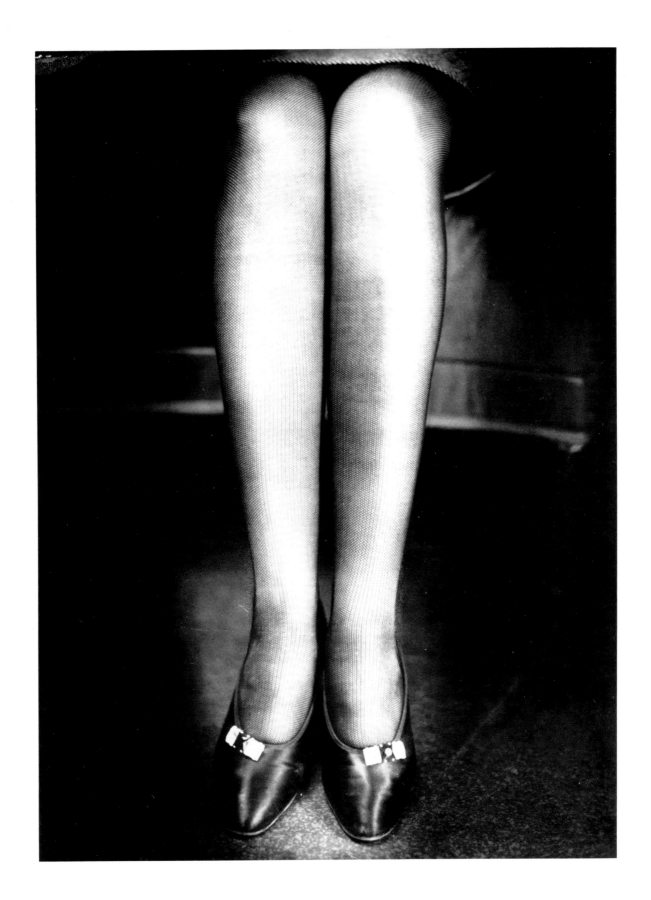

65   Yva, Untitled, 1929

66   Hans Finsler, Eggs, ca. 1930

67   Hans Finsler, Untitled, n.d.

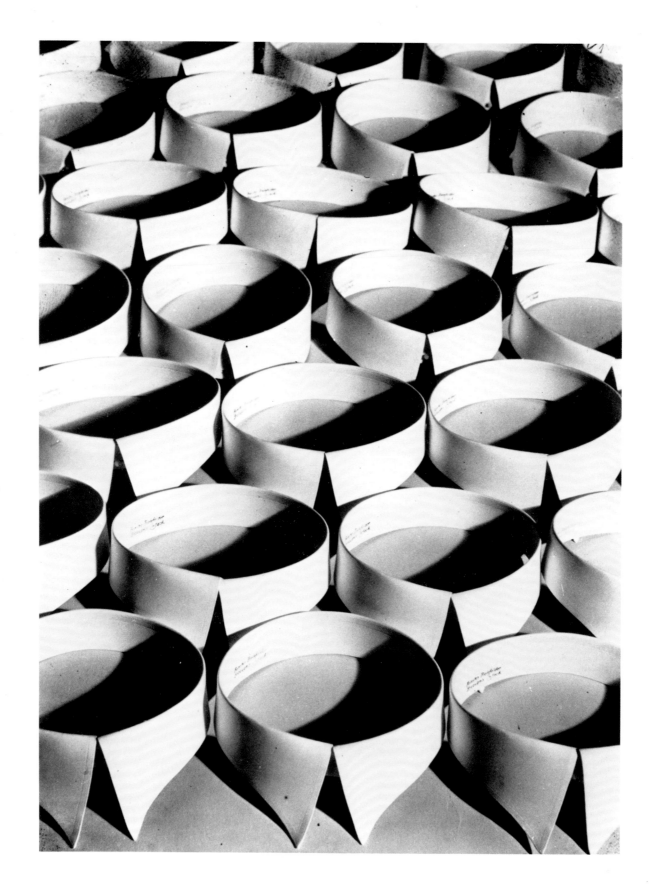

68   Hein Gorny, Untitled, ca. 1930

69   Hein Gorny, Untitled, ca. 1930

70   Albert Renger-Patzsch, Blast Furnace Herrenwyk, 1927

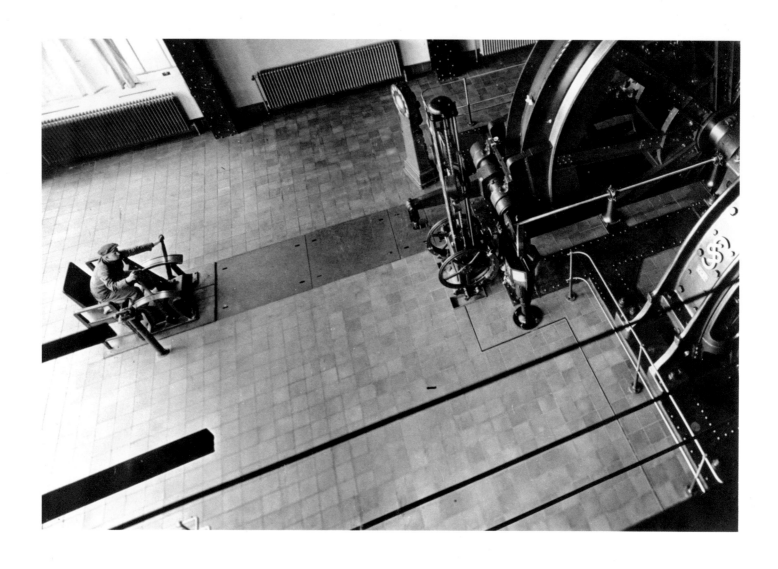

71   Max Burchartz, Working Place, ca. 1932

72   Felix H. Man, Steel Mill, 1929

73   László Moholy-Nagy, Railroad Bridge, Cologne 1927/29

74 Albert Renger-Patzsch, Railroad, n.d.

75   Alfred Ehrhardt, Shell, ca. 1932

76 Karl Blossfeldt, »Papaver Orientale«, n.d.

77   Karl Blossfeldt, »Cucurbita«, n.d.

78 Albert Renger-Patzsch, »Heterotrichum Macrodum«, 1922

79   Albert Renger-Patzsch, Euphorbia Grandicornis«, ca. 1922

80 Arvid Gutschow, Fields, ca. 1928

81   Alfred Ehrhardt, »Wattenmeer« (Flats), 1934

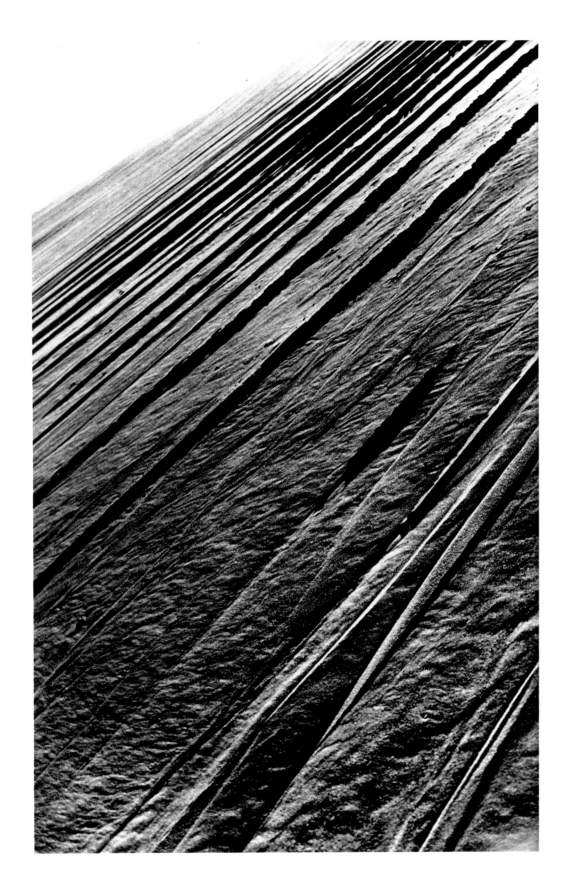

82   Alfred Ehrhardt, Dunes – Kurische Nehrung, 1936

83   Robert Petschow, Frozen River, n.d.

84 Robert Petschow, Balloon with Shadows, 1926

85 Hans Richter, »Vormittagsspuk« (Four Hats), 1927/28

86   Edmund Kesting, Untitled, ca. 1930

87   Herbert Bayer, Standing Objects, 1936

88   Herbert List, Lake Lucerne, 1936

89   Alice Lex-Nerlinger, Seamstress, 1930

90   Franz Roh, »Gross hängt die Winterwindsbraut in den Zweigen«, 1922/1926

91   Horacio Coppola, »Grandmother's Doll«, 1932

92   Herbert List, Untitled, London 1936

93 Georg Muche, »Composition«, 1922/23

94   Horacio Coppola, Egg and String, ca. 1932

95   Walter Peterhans, Untitled, n.d.

96   Sasha Stone, Untitled, ca. 1932

97   Hans Bellmer, Untitled, ca. 1937

98   Heinz Hajek-Halke, »Mirror Nude«, 1933

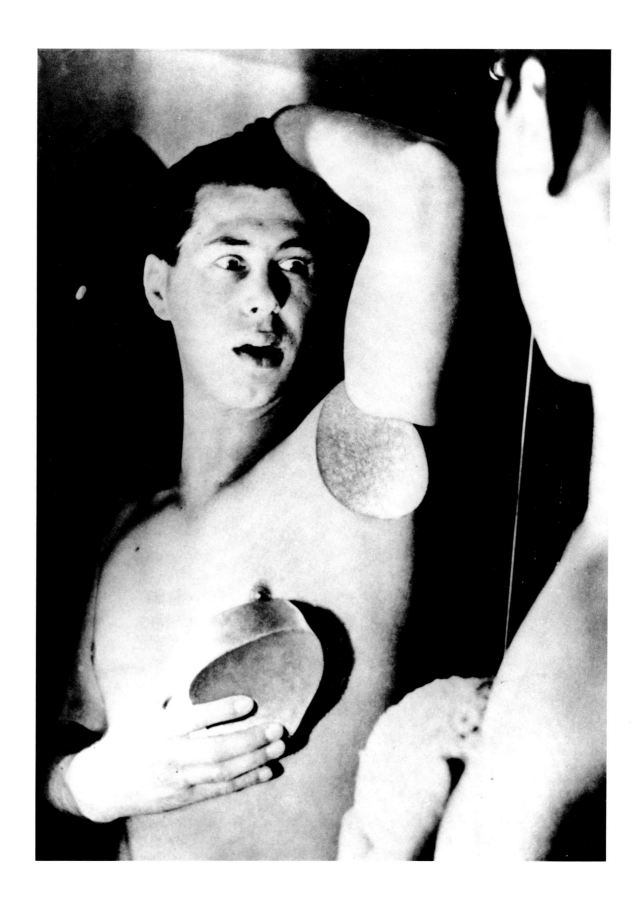

99   Herbert Bayer, Self-portrait, 1932

100   Andreas Feininger, »Nude II«, ca. 1935

101   Heinz Hajek-Halke, »Die üble Nachrede« (Vile Gossip), 1932

102 Klaus Wittkugel, Untitled, 1927

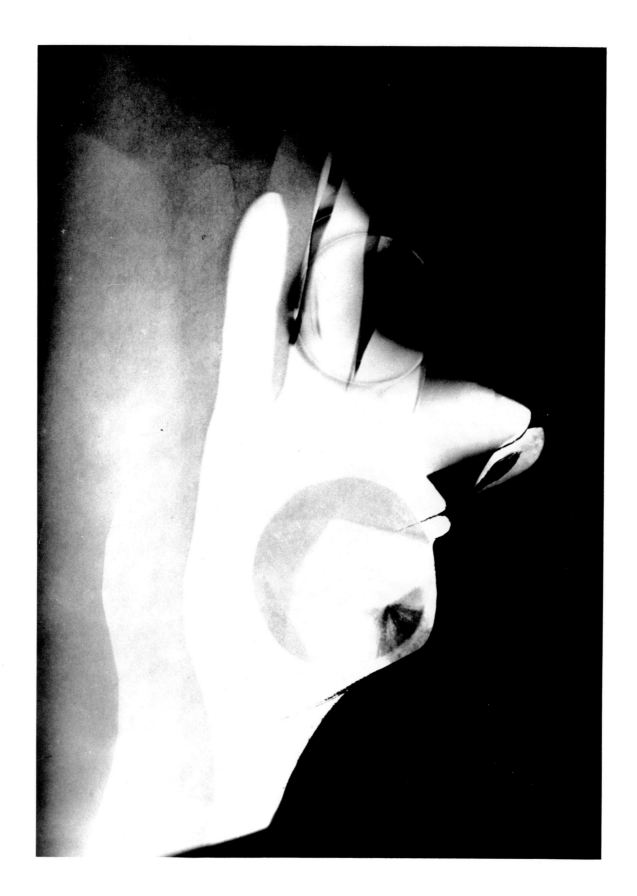

103   László Moholy-Nagy, »Rudolf Blümner«, 1922/23

104   Christian Schad, untitled, 1918

105   Willy Zielke, »Lichtreflexe«, n.d.

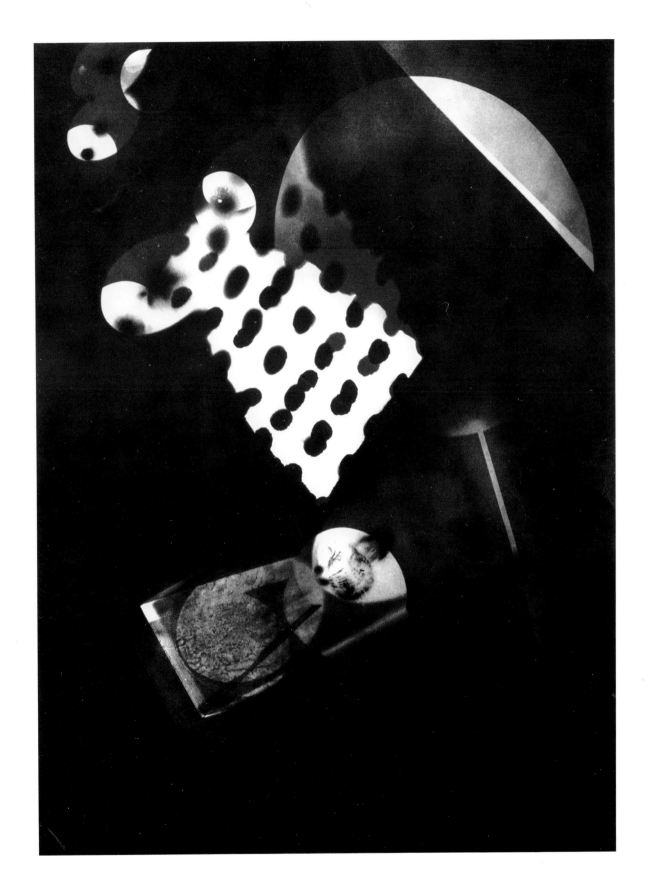

106   László Moholy-Nagy, Untitled, 1925

107   László Moholy-Nagy, »Broken Glass«, ca. 1936

108　Marta Hoepffner, »Hommage à Kandinsky«, 1937

PICTURE CREDITS

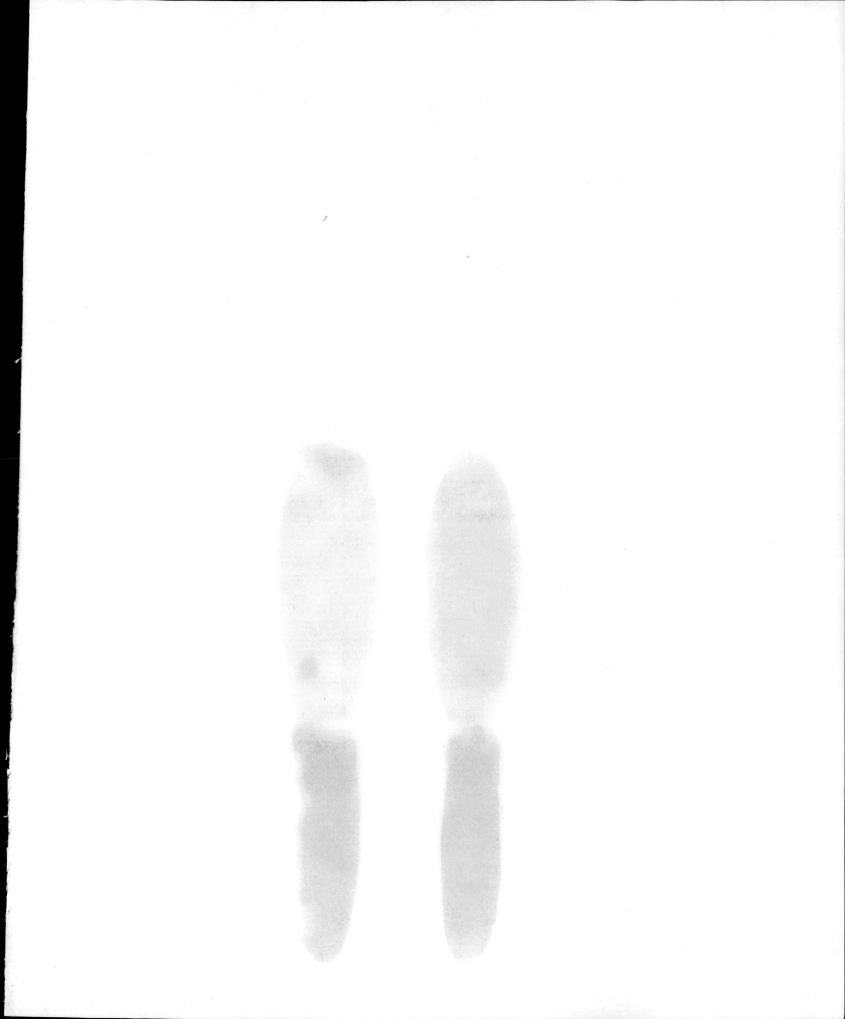